16980
821

Derek W erton H
ry R 1

SELECTED POEMS

Notes by Loreto Todd

MA (BELFAST), MA PH D (LEEDS)

Reader in International English, University of Leeds

LONGMAN
YORK PRESS

YORK PRESS
Immeuble Esseily, Place Riad Solh, Beirut

LONGMAN GROUP UK LIMITED
Longman House, Burnt Mill,
Harlow, Essex CM20 2JE, England
Associated companies, branches and representatives
throughout the world

First published 1993

ISBN 0–582–21536–6

Phototypeset by Gem Graphics, Trenance, Mawgan Porth, Cornwall
Printed in Singapore

Contents

Part 1

Introduction

The life and work of Derek Walcott

Derek Alton Walcott was born in Castries, St Lucia, on 23 January 1930. His mother was a teacher, his father a civil servant who painted and wrote poetry. He has a sister, Pamela, and a twin brother, Roderick Aldon. The parents' interest in language is apparent in the similarity of the boys' names, and an intense interest in language was to become one of the major characteristics of Derek's writing. The Walcotts were not typical St Lucians. They were middle class, Protestant and English-speaking in a community where most black people were poor, Catholic and spoke a French creole. Perhaps this separateness helps to account for the sense of loneliness and alienation that is another characteristic theme in Walcott's poetry and drama.

Derek Walcott's father died in 1931 and, although there were relatives who tried to compensate for this loss, Walcott frequently writes about the father he could not have known. He attended St Mary's College in Castries from 1941 to 1947 and held a post as assistant master there from 1947 to 1950. In 1948, he paid for the publication of his first volume of poetry, and showed his keen interest in the arts by co-founding the St Lucian Arts Guild in 1950. In the same year, Henri Christophe, a history play in verse, and his first experiment with drama, was published. Also in 1950, Walcott won a scholarship to the University College of the West Indies in Jamaica where he gained a B.A. and a Diploma in Education. In 1954, he got married, and taught for a year at his old school in St Lucia. A year later, however, he returned to Jamaica, where he combined teaching with writing for Kingston's *Public Opinion*. In 1957, he was commissioned to write a play, *Drums and Colours*, for a Trinidadian dramatic festival which was funded by a Rockefeller Foundation Grant. This was also the year in which he first visited the United States.

A Rockefeller Foundation Fellowship received in 1957 allowed Walcott to return to the US for a year to study theatre. When he returned to Trinidad, he founded the Little Carib Theatre Company, which was later renamed the Trinidad Theatre Workshop. Between 1959 and 1962, Walcott combined writing poetry and plays with a regular feature in the *Trinidad Guardian*, and his work began to be recognised. In 1960, he was married for the second time; in the same year, the Arts Advisory Council for Jamaica awarded him a prize for his innovatory approach to West Indian theatre; and a year later, he won the Guinness Award for Poetry for 'A Sea-Chantey', included in the collection *In a Green Night* (1962). Over the next 15 years, he continued to earn money as a journalist, and international fame and awards as a poet and playwright. Among the most significant of his awards were a Royal Society of Literature Award (1966), an OBE (1972), an honorary Doctor of Literature degree from the University of the West Indies (1973) and the Guggenheim Award (1977). In 1976, he resigned as Director of the Trinidad Theatre Workshop, and made his home more or less permanently in the US. In 1979, he became an Honorary Member of the American Academy of Arts and Letters in New York; in 1981, he became Professor of Creative Writing at Boston University; and in 1982, he was married for the third time. His stature was confirmed by the award of the Queen's Gold Medal for Poetry in 1988 and by the award of the Nobel Prize for Literature in October 1992.

Walcott has been writing poetry for more than 40 years, and in that time, he has produced over 300 poems of varying length. His first three volumes were written between the ages of 18 and 21, and were published at his own expense. These collections are *Twenty-Five Poems* (1948), *Epitaph for the Young* (1949) and *Poems* (1951). After a break of over ten years, his first publication that gave his work an audience in the wider world was *In a Green Night: Poems 1948–1960* (1962). Since then, a further nine volumes have appeared: *The Castaway and Other Poems* (1965), *The Gulf and Other Poems* (1969), *Another Life* (1973), *Sea Grapes* (1976), *The Star-Apple Kingdom* (1979), *The Fortunate Traveller* (1981), *Midsummer* (1984), *The Arkansas Testament* (1987) and *Omeros* (1990).

Walcott is widely recognised as one of the finest living poets writing in the English language. Many, perhaps, forget that he is also an innovative playwright whose theatrical talent was recognised early in the 1960s. His interest in plays, however, goes back much further than that. His earliest extant play, *Henri Christophe: A Chronicle in Seven Scenes*, was typed and mimeographed when he was a student in Jamaica in 1949, and modified and printed in 1950. Like the poetry which he was writing at the same time, it is influenced by Elizabethan writing, and particularly by such historical verse plays as Shakespeare's *Henry IV* (1596–8) and Christopher Marlowe's *Edward II* (1592). Walcott had faith in his own writing and funded the publication of *Henri Christophe* in 1950. The play proved successful and was staged, mainly for students, in St Lucia (1950), London (1952), Jamaica and Trinidad (1954), and it was broadcast by the BBC on *Calling the West Indies* in 1951.

Walcott's next complete play, *Harry Dernier* (1952), was another privately printed verse play. Although it was written as a radio play, and broadcast by the BBC, it was also staged by Walcott for a university audience in Jamaica. His third play, *The Charlatan*, probably written in 1954, is more ambitious and less derivative than his earlier works – a musical farce with Calypso elements. However, it remained unperformed until it was revised and given a world première in Los Angeles in 1974. His subsequent output has been prolific and other plays include: *The Sea at Dauphin* (1953), *Wine of the Country* (1953), *Ione* (1957), *Ti Jean and His Brothers* (1957), *Drums and Colours* (1958), *Malcauchon* (1958; later *Malcochon*), *Jourmard* (1959), *The Dream on Monkey Mountain* (1968), *In a Fine Castle* (1970), *Conscience of a Revolutionary* (1971), *The Joker of Seville* (1974), *O Babylon!* (1976), *The Snow Queen* (a television play, 1976), *Remembrance* (1977), *Pantomime* (1978), *Marie Laveau* (1979) and *A Branch of the Blue Nile* (1986).

Walcott's plays are interesting in their own right, but they are also of value in emphasising the literary themes that have preoccupied him at different times in his life. The plays begin with youthful verse drama; progress by using Caribbean music and folk motifs, including trickster heroes; and develop into vehicles for the examination of the role of writers and their plays in society.

Cultural and poetic background

Culture

In his poem, 'A Far Cry from Africa', Walcott describes the confusion of identity, almost schizophrenic in nature, that was experienced in his day by many people born in the Caribbean. The blood of both Europe and Africa ran in their veins; many of their cultural traditions were African, whereas their formal education was European in orientation. Their mother tongue overlapped with the language of their colonial masters, but it was permeated with African idioms and reflected an African world view. Walcott poses the problem in the form of a question:

I who am poisoned with the blood of both,
Where shall I turn, divided to the vein?
I who have cursed
The drunken officer of British rule, how choose
Between this Africa and the English tongue I love?

Walcott left the Caribbean to live, teach and write in the United States, leaving the islands where he had once felt at home, to live in a country where he was often left alone. Frequently, in his poetry, he expresses regret for following the exile's path north – 'I had abandoned them' (*The Arkansas Testament*) – and a sadness that he could not settle for human happiness – 'A girl smells better than the world's libraries' (*Omeros*). Yet the Caribbean formed him, and images of its sea and islands, its people and its traditions, its music and its history, infuse his writings. He left the islands to find his identity as a writer and, although the islanders wanted nothing from him, he has moulded himself so that he can leave them, as he tells us in *Omeros*, 'this thing that I have called "The Light of the World"'.

The language of the Caribbean, the creole formed from a fusion of European and African languages, is also an omnipresent force in his verse. At first, he uses the 'patois' to give expression to local idiom, but his use of it grows in quality and quantity until, in *The Fortunate Traveller*, it becomes a flexible medium for humour and satire, a verbal equivalent of musical Calypso.

Language

Walcott, like his poetic creation, Shabine, might have claimed:

> I have Dutch, nigger, and English in me,
> and either I'm nobody, or I'm a nation.
>
> ('The Schooner *Flight*')

Within his poetic register is a full repertoire of styles, reflecting the power and vitality of the English of Shakespeare and the King James Bible, the wit of John Donne and the Metaphysical poets, the epigrammatic precision of Alexander Pope, the lyricism of the Romantics, the creativity of James Joyce, the curiosity of Mark Twain and the homeliness and precision of Caribbean creole. Walcott read and learnt from British, Irish and American writers. Unconsciously, perhaps, he took Yeats's advice: 'poets, learn your trade,/Sing whatever is well made' ('Under Ben Bulben').

He also listened and learnt from Caribbean people whose ancestors had been enslaved, transported from Africa, and forced to learn pidgin languages which they transformed into communication systems that have been described and often disparaged as creoles, dialects, patois, but which are fully capable of verbalising, as Wordsworth put it:

> The still sad music of humanity,
> Nor harsh nor grating, though of ample power
> To chasten and subdue.   ('Tintern Abbey')

The mixed linguistic inheritance has proved to be the ideal medium for the subjects that have become thematic in his poetry. Commenting on the appropriateness of Walcott's Nobel Prize, Robert Winder focused on the poet's dual strengths: 'Standing astride the chasm between two cultures, he has found a toehold in the best of both worlds' (*The Independent*, 9 October 1992).

Themes

All writers of stature treat their material in original and stimulating ways.

They may see what we see, but they can express what they see with a clarity that allows us to see with new eyes. Many cultures are aware of the special gifts of creative artists. In parts of Africa, for example, storytellers are invited to 'See so that we can see; speak so that we can hear; show so that we can understand.' Writers do not, of course, see everything with equal clarity. Some subjects appeal to them more than others and these begin to recur in their work. Walcott shows an interest in a wide range of subjects, but the ones that appear in both his poetry and his plays are:

(1) the history of the Caribbean
(2) politics and their effect on people
(3) the sea around the Caribbean islands
(4) injustice
(5) the role of the artist in society
(6) the poet as a speaker for himself and as a spokesman for society
(7) the value of poetry to culture and society
(8) the passage of time
(9) the interaction of opposites:
> black and white
> home and exile
> joy and suffering
> life and death
> love and hate

In many of Walcott's poems, he uses these themes in combinations that highlight the effect of one on the other. As with his treatment of opposites, he derives a powerful irony from the understanding that one cannot recognise good without knowing evil, and love without knowing hatred. The effect is like that on Adam in the Bible, who begins to comprehend the meaning of immortality only when he accepts that he is mortal.

Influences

Walcott had read widely and absorbed many poetic influences, even by the time he was 18. The reading and the influences have continued throughout his life. He absorbed Shakespeare and Marlowe, Donne and Marvell, Milton and Pope, Wordsworth and Keats, Browning and Tennyson, Longfellow and Walt Whitman, Yeats and T. S. Eliot, Auden and Pound, Philip Larkin and Seamus Heaney. In addition, he read French poets, including Charles Baudelaire, Paul Verlaine, Stéphane Mallarmé, and black writers, such as Wole Soyinka and Aimé Césaire, from both Africa and the Caribbean. As well as the influences from published writers, came the inspiration from reggae and dub poetry. These varieties began to be recognised in the 1970s, especially in Jamaica. They are a fusion of oral and literary traditions, combining folk speech and popular music, and have informed political protest through the work of artists like Bob Marley. Walcott has forged his own style by his wide reading and listening. He has absorbed and then transformed all this material in a variety of ways to suit the subject matter of his verse. It is not easy to generalise about a poet who has written so much over such a long period, but we can point to three verse styles which characterise much of Walcott's poetry.

First, we find the iambic pentameter, lines which have five strong stresses, usually in the pattern unstressed–stressed, and often represented as: x / x / x / x / x /.

We find iambic pentameters in the measured verse of Shakespeare:

  x / x   / x   / x / x   /
  No longer mourn for me when I am dead
  x / x   / x / x / x /
  Than you shall hear the surly sullen bell . . . (Sonnet LXXI)

in the sonorous rhythms of Milton:

  x / x / x / x / x /
  When I consider how my light is spent
  x / x / x / x / x /
  Ere half my days in this dark world and wide . . .
              ('On His Blindness')

and in Walcott's 'The Gulf':

  x / x / x / x / x /
  above this cauldron boiling with its wars.

Often, especially in his mature writings, Walcott keeps the five stresses but introduces a variable number of unstressed syllables, giving his verse variety and a closer resemblance to the rhythms of ordinary speech:

  / x / x / x   / x /
  'This time, Shabine, like you really gone!'
  x / / x x / x / x / x
  I ain't answer the ass, I simply pile in . . .
            ('The Schooner *Flight*')

Secondly, Walcott often uses what we might describe as 'verse paragraphs' and 'free verse', also known as '*vers libre*'. He varies the rhythmical patterns, often avoids end-stopped lines and does not use capital letters to start a line, unless the line starts a new idea. There are many examples of verse paragraphs in *Another Life*. In Chapter 12, for example, there is a 27-line 'paragraph' in which only two of the lines begin with capital letters and 11 of them have no end stopping.

A third style that we might draw attention to is seen in poems such as 'The Swamp' in which we find short stanzas, usually of two, three or four lines, in which many of the lines contain as few as one (e.g. 'Ahead') or two words (e.g. 'Like death').

Although all three of these poetic styles are associated with a great deal of Walcott's poetry, none of them is unique to him. Even 'free verse', which is often thought of as modern, can be found in some of the Old Testament psalms. Nor is Walcott limited to one style in a poem. We can find pentameters or short lines in his free verse, just as we can find a tendency to avoid monotonous regularity even when he chooses to write a strictly controlled sonnet.

Reading Walcott

When we first come across a Walcott poem, it is like meeting people who speak a different language. We can guess at the meaning from things that are familiar to us, their gestures and facial expressions, but we are incapable of understanding their nuances. We have two possible responses: we can be satisfied with a superficial, partial understanding, or we can learn the language and participate in the communication. A thorough understanding of Walcott takes time and effort. He has put all his intellectual gifts into creating intricate, thought-packed poems, and it will take all our intellectual energy to unpack them.

Walcott's techniques can be described but they do not impose limits on his vision or restrictions on his creativity. He has learnt that a writer's art finds its fullest expression when it can be disciplined by his craft. This relationship is understood by Seamus Heaney, who made the point in a radio interview when he defined poetry as 'the love act between the art and the craft'.

Walcott has often been described as a 'difficult' poet, and it is true that we cannot skim the surface of his work and expect to understand or appreciate what he is saying. The more we read him, the more we think about what he is saying, and the more we appreciate that his poems are not literary titbits to be swallowed and forgotten. He believes that the poet has a serious role in society. He not only entertains; he educates. He describes and comments and invites interaction from his readers. There is no easy way into Walcott's poetry. The best way to understand him is to read him aloud, think about what he is saying, and not to feel discouraged if his meaning does not seem clear or simple. Second-class literature can be classified easily; first-class literature is unique and can only be understood in terms of itself, and in terms of the unique structures the artist produces. Walcott's poems may be compared with pebbles thrown into the water. The pebbles produce eddies which get bigger and bigger the longer we watch them. Walcott drops ideas into our minds which ramify as we think about them. The more we read, the better we will understand, but the total impact of some of his verse will only fully manifest itself when we have understood that his subject matter is humanity itself. Milton once took on the task of justifying 'the ways of God to man'; Walcott attempts to show the treatment of people by people. He chooses to do this by means of poetic structures which, as he has said, 'feel as if they still have the dew on them'. In other words, they are true to life but are marked by imaginative vigour and freshness.

Walcott refuses to accept any limitations on the nature or scope of poetry. In his view, all human acts and aspirations can be expressed at least as memorably in poetry as in the novel. In a newspaper interview in 1991, he staked poetry's claim to be the *porte parole* of society, and added:

> It's been sort of an imperialist colonial state. The novel came in, invaded every damn thing, grabbed what it could out of poetry – narrative, the third person – and poetry's been out there ever since.

His 300-page verse epic, *Omeros*, proved that the novel was not the only literary medium which could deal with passion and power, or develop characters that come alive on the page and live on in the memory.

A note on the texts

Some poets, such as Sylvia Plath or Philip Larkin, write relatively few poems; others like William Wordsworth or William Butler Yeats leave behind them 'high-pilèd books [which]/Hold like rich garners the full ripened grain' (Keats, 'When I have fears'). Derek Walcott, at the moment, comes somewhere in between, although his recent volumes, *The Arkansas Testament* and *Omeros* reflect the continuing expansion of his poetic world view into ambitious new areas, not often approached in poetry. In these volumes in particular, he is experimenting with the use of poetry for subjects like autobiography and philosophy, which are more usually treated in prose. The length and complexity of these recent poems puts them beyond the scope of these Notes. Yet, even when we restrict ourselves to the earlier volumes and shorter lyrics, we face the problem of variant forms. Walcott is a perfectionist. He writes and rewrites many of his poems and the modifications are not, necessarily, slight. If we look at the opening lines of the poem 'Sea Grapes', for example, we can illustrate this difficulty. In early 1976, they appeared in *American Poetry Review* as:

> That sail in cloudless light
> which tires of islands,
> a schooner beating up the Caribbean
>
> for home . . .

A month later, the *London Magazine* published:

> That sail, in cloudless, Sophoclean light
> which tires of islands

like any schooner beating up the Caribbean

archipelago home . . .

Four months later in the volume *Sea Grapes*, we read:

That sail which leans on light,
tired of islands,
a schooner beating up the Caribbean

for home . . .

The differences may seem small, but the versions of this 19-line poem reveal changes in punctuation, vocabulary, grammar and meaning. And these are not the only versions of the poem in existence. Such variety may indeed be 'the spice of life' but it can cause problems for commentators and readers. In order to ensure that we are thinking about the same version of a particular poem, I will comment on texts from three main sources:

Selected Poetry (Heinemann, 1981)
Caribbean Poetry Now (Hodder and Stoughton, 1984)
The Penguin Book of Caribbean Verse (Penguin, 1986).

It is worth emphasising, however, that variant forms of many poems do exist, and students may find these when studying different collections.

Part 2

Summaries
of POETRY COLLECTIONS

THIS SECTION offers a summary of each of Walcott's books of poetry written between 1948 and 1990. This is meant to give an idea of Walcott's total output, and to draw attention to some recurrent themes. Walcott paid $200 to publish his first volume of poetry, *Twenty-Five Poems*, in 1948 when he was 18. The 35-page booklet is clearly the work of a very young writer, influenced by poets such as W. H. Auden, John Donne, T. S. Eliot and Andrew Marvell, but we can already see in it themes that were to be explored and developed in later years: his interest in the sea and in islands, his attraction to the cultivated world of European art but also to ordinary people like 'The Fishermen Rowing Homeward', his knowledge of religion and his desire to comment on it, often in unexpected ways, as in 'Saint Judas'.

A year later, in 1949, he paid for the printing of his second volume of poetry, a 38-page booklet called *Epitaph for the Young: XII Cantos*. This time, the main influences were the Irish writer, James Joyce, and the Italian poet, Dante Alighieri. Dante wrote *The Divine Comedy* (1304), an allegorical account of a journey through Hell, Purgatory and Heaven, on which he was accompanied by the Latin poet, Virgil, and an idealised female companion, Beatrice.

In 1951, Walcott produced the third and last of his privately funded publications, a 46-page paperback, called *Poems*. It included 32 poems, several of which had been published in the Barbados periodical *Bim*. This volume shows how his subject matter was widening. There are verses dedicated to writers such as the American poet Hart Crane and to beautiful women, but there is also a growing interest in more serious subjects, such as the role of statesmen and the love-hate relationship between black and white, as symbolised in Shakespeare's play, *Othello* (*c.* 1604).

In 1962, *In a Green Night: Poems 1948-60* was published in London. It contained 42 poems, including a number of early attempts, as well as new ones, such as 'A Far Cry from Africa' in which he explores the troubled relationships between Europeans and Africans. The title of this volume shows his continuing interest in the Metaphysical poets. Andrew Marvell's poem 'Bermudas' contains the couplet:

He hangs in shades the orange bright,
Like golden lamps in a green night.

The poems also show a growing interest in life in the United States. His poem 'Bleeker Street', for example, deals with New York's Greenwich Village and can be usefully compared with the Simon and Garfunkel song 'Bleeker Street' (1970), which it predated and, to some extent, anticipated.

In 1964, his 85-page collection, *Selected Poems*, was published in New York. It was in three parts, Part 1 containing 23 poems which had appeared in *In a Green Night*, and Parts 2 and 3 made up of 16 poems written between 1960 and 1964. In one of them, 'The Glory Trumpeter', Walcott uses the persona of a trumpeter to examine how an artist can be associated with two cultures, without fully belonging to either. Eddie, the trumpeter of the title, literally turns his back on the Caribbean as he stands on the deck:

His horn aimed at those cities of the Gulf,
Mobile and Galveston . . .

In 1965, *The Castaway and Other Poems* was published in London. This volume of 27 poems shows a growing preoccupation with isolation: physical, racial, emotional and spiritual. The Robinson Crusoe-type castaway is a metaphor for the artist, especially the artist in words. The poet too is isolated, whether he is alone or surrounded by people, in the Caribbean or in the United States, but it is his self-appointed task to describe, even if he cannot explain, the duality of dependence and self-reliance. This volume also shows Walcott's continuing quest to understand the attraction and the repulsion which can characterise black–white interaction. The poem 'Goats and Monkeys' is based on Shakespeare's *Othello*, a play describing the tragic consequences of the suspicions between men and women, particularly when they are from different races. Othello murders his wife Desdemona and takes his own life because he believes the lies about her infidelity told by Iago. The poem is prefaced by a quote from Iago, in which he attempts to shock Desdemona's father by suggesting the unnaturalness of physical relations between black and white (Act 1, Scene 1).

Four years later, in 1969, came the 34 poems of *The Gulf and Other Poems*, which expands and develops many of the themes of *The Castaway*. The poem 'The Gulf', from which the volume takes its name, is literally meant as the Gulf of Mexico, but it becomes a metaphor for the many gulfs Walcott has become aware of: the gulf between the poet and both the cultures he has been exposed to; the gulf between black and white; the gulf between political aspirations and political expediency; the gulf between people and their roots.

After another four-year gestation period, *Another Life* was published in New York in 1973. Although it includes many of the themes we have come to expect from Walcott, it is different in form, style and theme from his earlier volumes. *Another Life* is an autobiographical sequence of 23 verse 'Chapters' in four sections: 'The Divided Child', 'Homage to Gregorias', 'A Simple Flame' and 'The Estranging Sea'. It is, in effect, a poetic evocation of the making of a 'Maker' or poet. It moves from childhood to maturity but its story is not chronological or naturalistically cohesive. Rather its sequence of events is realised through linked imagery and metaphor.

In 1976, *Sea Grapes* was published, a volume containing 46 new poems. To people not familiar with the bluish berries called 'sea grapes', the book's title is an unusual one, calling to mind the phrase 'sour grapes' as well as the painter's 'sea-scapes' and perhaps John Steinbeck's *The Grapes of Wrath* (1939), and reminding us of Walcott's love of the sea, especially the Caribbean Sea. One of the most memorable of the lyrics in this volume is 'Adam's Song'. Adam, the first man, experiences the link between love and life, and life and death. Adam's love song to Eve recognises that loving her will ensure his mortality, but it is a mortality that he freely chooses.

The Star-Apple Kingdom was published in New York in 1979. Like *Another Life*, it has an autobiographical element, but the personal details, thoughts, aspirations and achievements are percolated through the character of Shabine, a sailor, smuggler, poet and exile, who uses the creolised English of the Caribbean to express the yearnings of humanity:

I try to forget what happiness was,
and when that don't work, I study the stars.

Like *Sea Grapes*, the title is unusual, calling to mind 'magic kingdoms', 'castles in the air', W. B. Yeats's:

The silver apples of the moon
The golden apples of the sun . . .
　　　　　　　('The Song of Wandering Aengus' (1897))

and, most of all perhaps, the Greek myth about the daughters of Hesperus who, together with a dragon, watched over the garden of the golden apples in the Islands of the Blessed.

In 1981, *Selected Poetry* was published by Heinemann. The 50 poems were selected from *In a Green Night, The Castaway, The Gulf, Another Life, Sea Grapes* and *The Star-Apple Kingdom*, and they were edited and annotated by Wayne Brown, who is himself a poet. This volume gives a good idea of Walcott's development over a 20-year period, but has not been updated since first publication to include extracts from poetry written in the 1980s and 1990s.

The Fortunate Traveller (1981) is divided into three sections: 'I North', 'II South' and 'III North'. 'I North' contains five poems, 'II South' eighteen and 'III North' three. The dichotomy of north and south reflects the split between white and black, United States and Caribbean, rich and poor, conqueror and conquered. It draws attention to oppositions that need to be reconciled but avoids facile solutions or sentimental evasions. The verse in this volume makes use of Creole to explore and expound Trinidad's Calypso and to tackle serious issues, as in 'The Spoiler's Return':

we make them know they begging . . .
and giving gives us back the right to laugh
that we couldn't see we own black people starve,
and, more we give, more we congratulate
we-self . . .

Walcott's poetry has always included comments on the poet as a thinker and communicator, often depressed by the weight of human suffering. This subject matter is overt in a number of the poems in *Midsummer* (1984), including III:

Every word I have written took the wrong approach.
I cannot connect these lines with the lines in my face.

Midsummer contains 54 poems, each given a number from I to LIV, rather than a title. Only XLIII has a name, 'Tropic Zone', and it is composed of a further eight poems, numbered *i* to *viii*.

Like *The Fortunate Traveller*, published six years earlier, *The Arkansas Testament* (1987) is divided into two sections: 'Here' and 'Elsewhere'. The theme of the volume is the poet's 'homes' in the Caribbean islands, where he was born, and in the United States, where he has lived and worked since then. The division also reflects the biblical division of Old and New Testaments. 'Here' is, like the Old Testament, a record of the poet's birth, development and heritage; 'Elsewhere' is, like the New Testament, a more recent revelation of the experiences of a poet-prophet in a new land, the United States. The two 'testaments' are linked by the person of the poet, who is himself part black, part white, part African, part European, a microcosm of society, torn by social and racial inequalities. The poems in this volume explain the poet's message. They do it not directly, but through the mediation of a number of personas, dispossessed people, rushing to take the road 'from their galvanised hell'. The 'promise of salvation' of *The Arkansas Testament* is that people will look beyond the horizons that delimit their place of birth, and that the poet can leave people the only gift worth having – his art.

The long epic poem, *Omeros*, was published in 1990. It echoes Homer's *Iliad* in dealing with Caribbean characters with names like Achille, Helen, Hector and Philoctete. But its central character is the seemingly ageless, unaffectable sea:

O was the conch-shell's invocation, *mer* was
both mother and sea in our Antillean patois.
os, a grey bone, and the white surf as it crashes

and spreads its sibilant collar on the lace shore.
Omeros was the crunch of dry leaves, and the washes
that echoed from a cave-mouth when the tide has ebbed.

Omeros is divided into seven books, which are again split thematically
into two sections. The first three books relate the stories of some of the
St Lucian islanders. There are the fishermen, Achille, Hector and
Philoctete. Philoctete is injured by an anchor; Achille and Hector by their
quarrel over Helen. There is a blind prophetess and a wise woman, a pig
farmer, Plunkett, who studies history, and his wife, Maud, who traps island
birds in her embroidery. The last four books deal with exile and suffering,
followed by return, healing, a kind of understanding and reconciliation.
They examine a number of world cultures which may have influenced the
Caribbean and thus helped to create the characters and the complexities of
the region.

Part 3

Commentaries
on SELECTED POEMS

THIS SECTION comments on 50 poems, chosen from the works Walcott published between 1962 and 1992. These will be discussed in chronological order and a brief summary will be offered, followed by comments on words, phrases or imagery with which the reader may need guidance. A number of points need to be stressed at the outset. First, no short, prose summary can do justice to a poem. If poetry can, in part, be described as 'What oft was thought but ne'er so well expressed' (Pope, *Essay on Criticism* (1711)), then it is clear that the words selected by the poets are those that suit their purposes best. Secondly, a good poem defies simple definition. At one period of our life, it may say one thing to us, and at another, it may say something that is equally valid, but very different. It is as if the poet paints a word picture, which changes as we change our perspective. Thirdly, although a close study of the language of a poem will help us to understand it, it is only one stage in the poem's appreciation. We must read a poem, preferably aloud, to hear its word music; we must study its structures, thinking about how they interact and interrelate; we must evaluate the poem, asking ourselves why it attracts us; and we must not worry if our interpretation differs from someone else's. As the Welsh poet Dylan Thomas put it:

> You can tear a poem apart to see what makes it technically tick, and say to yourself, when the words are laid out before you, the vowels, the consonants, the rhymes and rhythms, 'Yes, this is *it*. This is why the poem moves me so. It is because of the craftsmanship.' But you're back again where you began. You're back with the mystery of having been moved by words. The best craftsmanship always leaves holes and gaps in the works of the poem, so that something that is *not* in the poem can creep, crawl, flash, or thunder in.*

The summaries of the poems below use the pronouns used by the poet. This is because Walcott pays close attention to the selection of pronouns, often using them ambiguously. He can, for example, use 'you' to refer to the reader(s) or to refer to himself and the reader(s) together in expressions like, 'You can get tired of things.' Where there is ambiguity, attention is drawn to this in the notes.

*Quoted in J. Scully (ed.), *Modern Poets on Modern Poetry*, Fontana Library, London, 1966, p. 202.

In a Green Night

'The Harbour'

SUMMARY:
Fishermen do not think about or value the calm water through which they row home. Neither do I seek the safety of an untroubled love, even though I know that stronger emotions may overpower me. There are many problems associated with erotic love: the lies, the deceit, the confinement. Others may watch my exploration of a more dangerous love, and may recognise the courage I show in facing a voyage of discovery where the new love (perhaps poetry) may behave with more cruelty than the sea. The final couplet suggests that those who are content with human love may travel in safety, and only hear rumours of the more daring who paddle out of their depth. The more adventurous lovers may be 'drowned', but will have seen the glory of the stars, so that death will have been freely chosen.

COMMENTARY AND NOTES:
'The Harbour' is a highly organised sonnet (a 14-line poem) in which a young man contemplates a choice between the pursuit of ordinary human love, *eros*, and the pursuit of a more spiritual form of love, *agapé*. We are not told much about the latter. It could be a search for spiritual enlightenment or, more likely, for the muse of poetry. Human love might provide peace, but it would be limiting. Art will provide stimulation, but may exact a heavy price. Walcott uses the sonnet form but uses a less rigid system of rhyme and rhythm. Instead of each line being a pentameter (i.e. having five strong syllables), the metre varies. Initially, too, it seems to have no rhyme, but a closer study reveals a pattern of half-rhymes: *a b a b c d c d e e f f g g* where 'dusk' (1.1) chimes with 'ask' (1.3). If we almost miss the rhyme scheme, we are unlikely to miss the alliteration involving 'f' ('fishermen', 'feelings', 'faring-forth', 'safe'), 's' ('dusk', 'consider', 'stillness', 'safe', 'stars' etc.), 'h' ('homeward', 'hands', 'humped hills', 'hoax', 'hearing') and 'w' ('homeward', 'winked', 'walls', 'watch', 'word', 'water'). The 'f's and 's's suggest friction and hissing; the 'h's and 'w's are uttered with a puff of air; so in this way the sounds of the poem echo and reinforce the images of the sea. Assonance too plays a major role in the poem. Walcott highlights the 'o' sound in 'rowing', 'homeward', 'no', 'knows', 'progress' and 'hoax', the 'i' sound in 'I', 'lies' and 'sly', and the long 'ay' sound in at least eight words including 'may', 'braving' and 'safe'.
Notice how we find linked sets of words and images in the poem. There are sets associated with the sea (e.g. 'fishermen', 'rowing', 'sea', 'watch', 'drowned'), with time (e.g. 'dusk', 'twilight', 'night', 'antique'), with the body (e.g. 'hands', tongue ('old lies'), eyes ('winked'), ears ('hear') and

legs ('climb')), and with emotions (e.g. 'feelings', 'love', 'calm'). These words and images are linked not only by meaning but by patterns of sounds.

The Harbour: this is literally a place of safety and refuge. Metaphorically, it is a place of spiritual safety during the voyage of life

since feelings drown: since emotions can overpower

no more ask: this has two possible meanings, 'no longer ask' and 'emphatically not ask'

urger of old lies: night is often associated with human love. It is a time for making promises that others have made, and broken, in the past

Winked . . . hills: the stars that have stood guard over the earth have seen lovers and their behaviour many times. 'Winked' has the double meaning of 'blink, twinkle' and 'connive at'. From sea level, the stars seem to be just above the hills. There is almost certainly a covert sexual reference in the alliterative phrase 'humped hills'

That . . . sea: the adventure of love which often involves deceit and which can be bitter as well as sweet

love raises walls: loving one person automatically means excluding and thus not loving others

Yet others . . . love: people who see the young man set out on his journey of self-analysis or search for artistic fulfilment may realise that he will experience more pain than those who are content with human love

antique hoax: old deception. Others have sought the enlightenment he seeks and either not found it, or found that, ultimately, it did not satisfy. Human yearning for the unattainable is probably as old as humanity itself. That is why the adjective 'antique' is selected

the secure from thinking: people who do not think too deeply may travel on 'liners', ships which will provide a comfortable journey through life

paddlers: people who devote themselves, even in a small way, to exploring life for themselves. 'Paddlers' may refer to people who play in shallow water or to small vessels guided by paddles or light oars

drowned near stars: they may be overcome by the elements they have challenged, but they will get near the stars, which provide both light and guidance and which symbolise beauty

'To a Painter in England'

SUMMARY:
I write from a tropical island to tell you, my friend, who are enduring an English winter in an English city, how I have grown to understand the painter's love of landscapes. It is April, and spring flowers will be appearing in England while there is drought and oppressive heat in the Caribbean. Walking near scenes that you have painted and encouraged me to paint, I saw small boats with un-English names and they remind me of your skill and reinforce my awareness of my inadequacy as a painter. Yet we both share a vision, which one can reveal in paint and the other in words. It is a vision which is felt as deeply as a religious experience, and which can be stimulated by either the natural or the supernatural.

COMMENTARY AND NOTES:
This meditative poem is written in five stanzas of unequal length (6, 7, 9, 9 and 7 lines respectively). There is little overt rhyme in the poem, but if we listen carefully to it, we will find assonance in 'explain', 'passionate' and 'landscape', and in 'parks' and 'branch'; we will notice the alliterative half-rhyme in 'burns', 'leaves' and 'names', and in 'drought' and 'quiet'. As the poet comes to terms with his strengths as well as his weaknesses, we find more overt rhymes in 'painting' and 'learning', in 'palette' and 'explicit', and, most obvious of all, in the final stanza, in 'whose' and 'refuse', in 'vision' and 'decision' and in 'thrush' and 'flesh'. There is an interesting shift of focus in the poem. It begins with an adverse comment on England's cold, dank, foggy cities, and switches to the light and warmth of the West Indies, only to turn then to emphasise the physical dryness, which seems to mimic his own artistic aridity. Although this is not a religious poem, it contains a number of words which can have religious connotations: 'talent', 'rails', 'season', 'ashes' (Ash Wednesday), 'dust' (Remember man that thou art dust . . .), 'St Mary Magdalen', 'gift', 'virginal', 'zeal', 'grace', 'vision', 'Sabbath', 'soul', 'cathedrals', 'love', 'the blind', (the word made) 'flesh'. Perhaps until poets can create their own mystical vocabulary, they tend to fall back on the language of religion.

personal islands: the meaning of this phrase exists on at least two levels. The islands of the West Indies have personal associations for the friend and the phrase reminds us of a famous passage in John Donne's *Devotions* XVII (1624): 'No man is an island, entire of itself'

Gauguins: painters like the French post-impressionist, Paul Gauguin (1848–1903), who left Europe to paint in the West Indies and Tahiti

sicken: grow sick with longing

April: Walcott chooses the month partly because of its associations in poetry. Robert Browning wrote: 'O to be in England now that April's here' ('Home Thoughts, from Abroad' (1845)) and T. S. Eliot wrote: 'April is the cruellest month' ('The Wasteland' (1922))

who will . . . pipes: who try to hide the fact that they are happy and want to sing

the tide burns/Black: where even the sea is so hot that it burns everything it touches. Walcott stresses the negative side of the Tropics in the Dry Season by suggesting that the water, which usually cools, can seem to burn things to a cinder. He is expressing the 'pathetic fallacy' which suggests that nature reflects our moods. He is experiencing artistic aridity, and so nature is also seen as arid with tides not wetting but burning, with leaves cracking, and with roads dusty

St Mary Magdalen: according to Christian tradition, Mary Magdalen was a prostitute who washed Christ's feet with her tears and dried them with her hair

soft villa: this is an unusual combination, in that we might expect a villa to be 'new' or 'neglected' but not 'soft'. It is an example of a transferred epithet, that is an adjective transferred from a person to a thing. When we talk about a 'sad farewell' or a 'happy meeting', it is the people who are happy or sad. In this poem, the instruction was 'easy' or 'soft'. A clear example of a transferred epithet occurs in the first stanza of Thomas Gray's 'Elegy Written in a Country Churchyard' (1751): 'The ploughman homeward plods his weary way.' It is the ploughman who is weary

Discloses . . . refuse: when we turn a corner, we may see a beautiful church and we can admire its beauty, whether or not we accept Christian teachings

hermit: hermits were early Christian recluses. The word is applied to a bird or animal that seems to prefer solitude

blind world: the world that is often indifferent to beauty

flesh: in the prayer the Angelus, we find the claim 'The Word was made flesh', meaning that God assumed our human nature and became a man. In a similar way, poets try to put 'flesh' on ideas so that these ideas can be shared

'A Far Cry from Africa'

SUMMARY:
Africa is changing. The Kikuyu people are becoming stronger. There is death and destruction in a continent that could be a paradise for all the people in it. People may list the number of dead Africans but do their many deaths compensate for the life of a white child? Hunters and their beaters prey on animals that have existed in Africa since the dawn of time. Animals often live by killing other animals. That is a law of nature. Man alone inflicts pain for its own sake and glories in war, irrespective of the numbers that die. Once again, we can find excuses for our behaviour; compassion is wasted; people from Africa are locked in a struggle with people from Europe. I have the blood of both races in my veins, so to which side do I owe allegiance? I can condemn the evil in British rule, but how do I choose between my African and my English heritage? How can I see the slaughter in Africa and remain indifferent?

COMMENTARY AND NOTES:
The title can be read both literally and idiomatically. Literally, it can mean 'being far from Africa and being sad', and 'a cry from Africa that is heard in the distance'. Idiomatically, it implies 'distant and different from Africa'. The poet empathises with African suffering, but is far away from Africa in terms of miles, upbringing and heritage. This is one of the earliest poems in which Walcott describes his dual inheritance. The poem is beautifully constructed in three metrically simple, rhymed stanzas. The vocabulary has a high component of words that we associate with Africa ('Kikuyu', 'veldt', 'savages', 'beaters', 'ibises', 'drum', 'gorilla') and also with suffering and death ('bloodstreams', 'corpses', 'worm', 'carrion', 'dead', 'hacked', 'cries', 'violence', 'pain', 'worried', 'waste', 'compassion', 'poisoned', 'slaughter'). Walcott uses irony in this poem. He does not approve of a white child being hacked to death, of Africans or Jews being 'expendable', of Africans being thought of as 'savages' or 'gorillas'. He puts such ideas down to shock us into a realisation of the cruelty that one set of human beings can inflict on another.

wind:	this is a reference to the 'winds of change' speech, made in South Africa in 1960 by the British Prime Minister, Harold Macmillan, in which he claimed that Africa was changing and governments would have to move in response to the demands of the people
tawny:	light brown, brownish
pelt:	hide of an animal
Kikuyu:	a tribe in Kenya, associated with the Mau Mau uprising in the 1950s
quick:	fast, alive, lively

Batten: thrive at the expense of someone else
veldt: open grasslands, usually in South Africa. The word is from Afrikaans and comes from the same root as 'field'
colonel: high-ranking officer
carrion: dead and rotting flesh
salients: points of defence in enemy-held territory; the most striking features
expendable as Jews: no more worthy of saving than the six million Jews murdered by the Nazis
threshed: separated the grain from the husk, beat
ibises: tropical wading birds
beast-teeming: full of animals
Delirious: wildly, almost madly, excited
carcass of a drum: drum made by stretching an animal's skin over a frame
white peace: (1) a peace created by whites and not worthy of the name; (2) in death, black skins appear much lighter
Spain: this is a reference to the Spanish Civil War (1936–9) when fascists fought socialists
The gorilla wrestles with the superman: the African struggles with the technically superior European

'Ruins of a Great House'

SUMMARY:
Walcott meditates on the ruins of a mansion, once built by a slave-owner. The beautifully dressed girls who once lived in the house have disappeared; the gateway carvings are stained; and the trappings of wealth are covered with dirt. Three crows settle on a tree. There is the living smell of eucalyptus and lime trees and the metaphorical smell of a decaying empire. There was once great beauty here and the stones have survived the people who brought them, and who now lie buried in the grounds. The slave owners are gone and the passage of time helps one to forget the pain. The people who owned the house and the people who served in the house have all gone and the edifice is crumbling, just as the Empire has decayed. Slave traders like Sir John Hawkins and Sir Francis Drake came to this part of the world. So did the poet and adventurer, Sir Walter Raleigh. There was beauty and cruelty, suffering and courage, and time makes us see the transience of it all.

COMMENTARY AND NOTES:
The quotation at the beginning of the poem is taken from the treatise *Urn Burial*, written by Sir Thomas Browne in 1658. In it, he examines the

various methods used to dispose of the dead, and meditates on human mortality. This poem is in a long tradition of verse often summed up by the Latin tag, *Sic transit gloria mundi* ('Thus passes the glory of the world'). It is characteristic of Walcott that he juxtaposes opposites, slave-owner and slave, the brevity of human life and the lasting quality of the edifices humans erect, the rise and fall of empires, and the fact that good and bad can co-exist in the same individual.

The 51 lines of this poem are divided into nine unequal sections of 6, 4, 2, 6, 4, 7, 11, 8 and 3 lines, possibly to reinforce the non-traditional response to his subject matter. Notice how most of the first 14 lines are end-stopped, each line containing a word picture. There are no fixed patterns of sound, just as there are no judgments. We find half-rhyme in 'claws', 'trees', 'boughs' and 'nose'; eye rhyme in 'stone' and 'gone'; assonance in 'dust' and 'muck'. It is as if the poet is attempting to forge his ideas and is not, at first, aware of the reason for past behaviour. The central section, between lines 15 and 29, moves more freely, untrammelled by much end-of-line punctuation, reflecting the poet's thoughts as they take in life and death, temporal and religious empires. From line 30 onwards, the ideas, like the structure, are more regimented. Notice the increased use of full rhyme, 'next', 'perplexed' and 'text', 'thought' and 'fought', 'deranged' and 'arranged'. Finally, and surely intentionally, we find 'ends' and 'friend's'. Death treats everyone alike.

Ruins of a Great House: the title sets the tone of the poem. We expect it to include details of disintegration, former wealth and an awareness of 'How the mighty are fallen!'

Stones: Shakespeare begins Sonnet LXV (1609) with 'Since brass, nor stone, nor earth, nor boundless sea,/But sad mortality o'ersways their power', and comments on the fact that nothing can withstand the ravages of time, except perhaps poetry

disjecta membra: scattered remains

moth-like girls: (1) girls who are dressed in flimsy, gossamer-like gowns; (2) girls who are attracted to bright lights, even though the attraction will be their undoing

gate cherubs: stone ornamental angels sometimes carved over the gates of large country houses

Three crows: crows are depicted as birds of prey and carrion crows can survive on dead animals. There are many reasons for choosing 'three' crows, including the fact that three is a mystical number. In a poem like this, however, which can be compared to works by the Latin poet, Horace, Anglo-Saxon poets, Shakespeare, Donne and Blake, it is likely that Walcott is remembering the anonymous ballad, 'The Three Crows' (fifteenth century), in which the crows wait for a young knight to die

eucalyptus: trees cultivated for the sweet-smelling, medicinal oil in their leaves

limes: citrus trees

quickens: there is a pun here. The word can mean 'speeds up' or 'brings to life'. It is so close to 'lime' that we are also meant to think of 'quicklime' which was used to catch birds, to improve a land's fertility and to help bodies, especially the bodies of criminals, to decompose quickly

leprosy: an infectious disease that is marked in its early stage by its sweet smell and by the white patches that appear on the skin. Leprosy eventually causes disfigurement and wasting of the affected parts

Farewell, green ... groves: there are many allusions to writers in this poem. These lines are from the English poet William Blake who wrote a number of very well-known poems, including 'The Little Black Boy' (1789), in which an African child speaks about the long-term insignificance of the colour of one's skin

Marble as Greece: marble such as was used in ancient Greece. Marble is a crystalline form of limestone

Faulkner: William Faulkner (1897–1962) was an American novelist who wrote about the American 'Deep South', where there was a considerable amount of racial hatred

Deciduous: impermanent, transitory. The adjective is usually applied to trees that lose their leaves in autumn

imperious rakes: disreputable young men, usually from the upper echelons of society. Often such men were sent to the colonies so that they would not disgrace their families

padded cavalry: the soft feet of many mice. In American films, the cavalry often came to the rescue of the hero. There is no rescue from the ravages of time

Kipling: Rudyard Kipling (1865–1936) wrote poetry and prose, mainly about India. He was aware that racial and social differences were superficial: 'the colonel's lady and Rosie O'Grady/Are sisters under the skin.' He realised that the British Empire would die, just as all previous empires had

by Bible: Walcott is suggesting that missionaries as well as soldiers helped to establish the Empire, but also often hurt the people they attempted to convert

Hawkins ... Drake: Sir John Hawkins (1532–95) was an adventurer. He was involved in the Slave Trade and achieved fame for his part in defeating the Spanish Armada in 1588. Sir Walter Raleigh (*c.* 1554–1618) was an explorer, a courtier and a poet, who was executed on the orders of James I. He introduced potatoes and tobacco into Britain. Sir Francis Drake (*c.* 1540–96) sailed around the world and commanded the fleet that defeated the Armada. These men of action, admired in Britain, were all involved in cruel activities in the Caribbean

charnel galleon: a ship that carried dead bodies out to sea for burial

rot remains: an oblique reference to Shakespeare's play, *Julius Caesar* (1599), where Mark Antony, speaking at Caesar's funeral, claimed: 'The evil that men do lives after them;/The good is often interred with the bones'

Donne: John Donne (*c.* 1572–1631) was a priest and poet who wrote a number of sonnets on death, including 'Death, be not proud'

coal of my compassion: the material that could cause compassion to express itself for a long time

Albion: an old name for Britain. England was sometimes referred to as 'perfidious Albion'. 'Albion' comes from Latin 'albus', meaning 'white'

colony: Britain was once a colony of Rome

part ... main: in a famous passage in his *Devotions* XVII (1624), John Donne wrote: 'No man is an island, entire of itself . . . every man is a piece of the continent, a part of the main'

Nook-shotten, rock o'erblown: containing many hiding places, visited by rooks, omens of death. These phrases are archaic and reminiscent of Old English poetry where the 'Hwær cwom' ('Where have they gone') genre lamented the fact that even the mighty died

All in compassion ends: a phrase reminiscent of the adage 'To know all is to forgive all'

'as well ... friend's': the line is taken from John Donne, *Devotions* XVII (1624); see note above on 'part . . . main'

'Tales of the Islands'

SUMMARY:
This poem consists of ten sonnets, which Walcott calls 'Chapters'. Each sonnet Chapter can be read and understood on its own but they are linked

by the common theme of stories about the West Indian islands. The first Chapter presents the islands as idyllic, but the following eight all focus on the decay, falseness and insanity behind this idyll. The final Chapter shows the youth leaving the islands, his rose-tinted view of his homeland an ironic statement that only distance can preserve the idyll.

Chapter I looks at the Dorée (gilded) river flowing through tree-lined gorges which makes the poet think of schools and cathedrals, of children and saints, and of the future possibilities of the young black people of the island.

Chapter II takes a section of the French National Anthem as its motif. 'Qu'un sang impur . . . ' is part of a line which prays that 'no impure blood' may cross the thresholds of France. Cosimo de Chrétien (Christian) ran a boarding house but was under his mother's thumb. Their home showed relics of former grandeur but the passage of time had diminished them.

Chapter III, subtitled 'La belle qui fut . . .' ('The beautiful woman who fled'), describes the now impoverished Miss Rossignol ('Nightingale') who lives in a home for poor Catholic ladies. She had once lived in splendour but had lost her wealth and her only child.

Chapter IV, 'Dance of Death', describes a visit to a brothel, where, in the strange light, everyone and everything looked green. The poet is struck by the fact that the dead far outnumber the living, and is gently mocked for philosophising in such a place, at such a time.

Chapter V, 'moeurs anciennes' ('ancient/former customs'), describes a ritual put on for some anthropologists. A lamb was sacrificed and its blood drunk. The sonnet uses the idiom of speech, describing the rite as one remembered from Africa, but its Christian significance is also apparent.

Chapter VI uses a variant of the creole to describe another fête, when there was free food and drink and steel band music. There is amusement that an educated man discusses Shelleyan angst while his wife may be having a good time along the beach, not far from where a child was supposed to have been ritually sacrificed a long time before.

Chapter VII, 'Lotus eater . . .', harks back to Alfred Lord Tennyson's poem, 'The Lotos-Eaters' (1832), where a group of mariners choose a life of languorous ease in exile in preference to the hardships of facing the sea and sailing home. In this sonnet, Franklin, gripped by malaria, knows that he too will only be able to dream of home.

Chapter VIII looks at another exile, a Jew perhaps, who lives in squalor in a little hotel. He has pamphlets that are collecting dust and he clutches a journal as life goes on around him, as oblivious to him as he seems to it.

Chapter IX, 'Le loupgarou' ('The werewolf'), considers Le Brun, another example of a white settler who has fallen on hard times. He is now old and ill. The story goes that he turned into a werewolf one night and was seriously wounded by his own watchman when he returned home.

Chapter X, 'Adieu foulard . . .' ('Goodbye silk scarf'), deals with a young person leaving the island, looking at it from his plane and foolishly hoping that nothing on the island will change.

COMMENTARY AND NOTES:
Each 'Chapter' is a sonnet but they vary considerably in terms of their formal characteristics. They all employ variations on the pentameter line: 'The /marl white /road, the /Dorée /rushing /cool' (I); and all use rhyme: '13' and 'barquentine' (II); half-rhyme: 'lazaretto' and 'Donatello' (III); alliteration: 'Greco', 'Goya', 'girls', 'good' and 'green' (IV); and assonance: 'fête', 'place', 'lead' and 'grace' (V); but it is only in the final sonnet that the poet submits to the rigours of fixed metre and patterned rhyming.

Chapter I
marl: fine-grained soft rock, consisting of clay minerals and silt
ici: here, here is
Choiseul: place-name
Via Dolorosa: from Latin meaning 'sorrowful road'. The term is applied to the route followed by Christ from the home of Pontius Pilate to Mount Calvary. It is also sometimes used for an arduous journey or trying experience
Sancta Teresa: St Teresa of Avila (1515–82) was a Spanish noblewoman who became a Carmelite nun and who wrote about her mystical experiences in *The Way to Perfection*. She has been the subject of many paintings and of a Baroque sculpture by Giovanni Bernini, which inspired a poem by the English Metaphysical poet, Richard Crashaw

Chapter II
maman: French children's name for 'mother'
perroquet: parrot
barquentine: a sailing ship with three or more masts
ikon: more usually spelt 'icon' (and appears as such in some editions); a religious image

Chapter III
Rossignol: nightingale
lazaretto: poorhouse, often for lepers
Magdalen of Donatello: like the thin, emaciated Mary Magdalen of the Italian sculptor Donatello (*c.* 1386–1466)
paupered: had made destitute

Chapter IV

epileptic: a person who loses consciousness periodically, often having a convulsion at the same time. Epilepsy was sometimes associated with sanctity

El Greco: 'the Greek', the painter Domenico Theotocopoulos (1541–1614), noted for the elongated figures that appear in his work

Goya: Francisco José de Goya (1746–1828) was a Spanish painter, best known for his portraits and depiction of war

the trade: prostitution

the quick: the living

the wages . . . is birth: Walcott parodies the biblical quotation which is 'The wages of sin is death'

Chapter V

fête: feast, a saint's anniversary or feastday

black customs: there is an ironic equation between 'savage rites' and 'black customs'. Walcott is drawing attention to the fact that many 'white' scholars assume that all African customs are savage. He then point out that there is a remarkable similarity between this ritual and the ritual underlying the sacrifice of the Mass

Chapter VI

Poopa: term of respect to an older man

I mean . . . edgewise: this long, conversational, mainly unpunctuated passage is meant to represent the flow of apparently unstructured ideas

Shelley: Percy Bysshe Shelley (1792–1822) was an English Romantic poet whose wife wrote *Frankenstein* in 1818

Chapter VII

urine-stunted: it is believed that urine can damage plants

breed: Shakespeare concludes his Sonnet XII (1609), which deals with the inevitability of death, with the couplet: 'And nothing 'gainst Time's scythe can make defence/Save breed, to brave him when he takes thee hence'

Chapter VIII

Falangists: members of the fascist party founded in Spain in 1933, supporters of General Franco

en la guerra civil: in the Spanish Civil War

bleeding . . . dew: a religious reference. There were a number of reports

	of the sun bleeding while people prayed on their rosary beads
caballo:	horseman
sunwashed:	blend of sun and unwashed

Chapter IX

loupgarou:	werewolf
threaded:	Walcott uses a pun here to suggest that the story was passed on by the 'greying' women who met together to sew
jalousies:	Venetian blinds, but there is also a suggestion of 'jealousies'
Pink glasses:	glasses worn by the blind or perhaps by people suffering from 'pink eye' or acute conjunctivitis
cork hat:	there may possibly be a pun here on 'cocked hat' or tricorn. 'Cork hats' are sometimes associated with the dead
lycanthrope:	werewolf. The word derives from Greek and is also a psychological term which can be applied to someone who thinks he is a wolf

Chapter X

fine/Writing of foam:	the sea's marks round the island remind the poet of handwriting
twine:	thin string
islets:	small islands
fuselage:	the main body of the plane

'A Careful Passion'

SUMMARY:
Two lovers sit at a table of an inn. They half listen to the music and the speaker's eyes are on the sea, rather than on his love. He thinks about the differences between this island and other islands to the south, between this love, who is married, and an earlier love. They can no longer communicate so he allows memories to fill his mind. The apparent happiness of the gulls emphasises their estrangement. He suggests that they should break up before they get hurt, and the clichéd expression comes out easily in the languid atmosphere of the bar. He strokes her hand to counteract the brusqueness of the words. It seems better to pretend to some feeling that he no longer has. It seems the civilised thing to do, even though the well-worn phrases indicate the shallowness of his feeling. The clichés do, in fact, express the truth. Love affairs like this may begin with exhilaration, but they are doomed. They walk off together as night begins to fall, aware of many things, but not of each other.

COMMENTARY AND NOTES:
The title is unusual, almost a paradox, in that passion is normally assumed to be ardent, intense, spontaneous, not 'careful'. There is, however, a degree of calculation in the young man's ardour.

The poem has, as its foreword, a quotation from a Jamaican spiritual which praises God even when he seems to mock human efforts. The significance of the quotation is that human love may not even last as long as the house which is washed away by the rain.

As in many of Walcott's poems, the stanzas are of unequal length (7, 12, 10, 5, 9 and 4 lines respectively), with each showing a complex rhyming system. The word and the rhyme 'edge' are common to each stanza. They are at the edge of the city, not too close to the harbour's edge; their table is near the water's edge; and the gulls search the sea's edge. The repetition suggests that their relationship has never been very intense, that they stood at the edge of passion. We see the relationship through the man's eyes. We learn little about the woman, except that her hand drummed in time to the music, that her hand wore her husband's ring, that she allowed her hand to be stroked, that his words brought tears to her eyes. There is a strong possibility that she may not have wanted the affair to end.

Marimba:	Latin American percussion instrument
You:	one, a person
silts:	clogs. It is easier to indulge in memories than to face the difficulties of the present
sun-puffed carcass:	speaks of himself almost as if he were dead. This is an unpleasant image, suggesting pride and physical corruption
cha cha cha:	a Latin American dance. The lively rhythms mock the stagnation of the relationship
I walk with her:	notice that the focus is on the narrator. The relationship might have endured if they had walked together

'Castiliane'

SUMMARY:
The hotel is ugly except for its ironwork, which many have found attractive. Yet even the wrought iron is no shield to the odours coming from the port. In a type of daydream, I have created a beautiful Spanish spirit woman, Donna, who is almost a montage of carvings and drawings and embroideries that I have seen. I wonder why she is only seen by me, why she hides from others, why she can summon up memories of Spain's Moorish history. As I wonder, a pigeon flies past and the odours of the street break into my reverie. I imagine the places this frail Donna may have seen, the music she would have heard, her father, her lover and her chaperones. The smell of the sea makes me wonder who would have won

the hand of his frail ghost. Perhaps she would have married a gold-toothed merchant and, if so, she would have been wise, because no one can live on poetry. And yet, she keeps coming back into my mind and helps me overlook the squalor of my surroundings.

COMMENTARY AND NOTES:
'Castiliane' is in three sections, each containing two stanzas. The stanzas are unequal in length but they are linked by a design pattern that is as intricate as the wrought-iron balcony of 1.3. Notice, for example, that the final word of the first and last lines of the poem is 'hotel'; that the repetition of particular words emphasises the structure including 'balcony', 'century', 'sea', 'guitar(s)' and 'weep(s)'; and that there is a considerable amount of 'feminine rhyme' where two or more syllables rhyme as in 'architecture' and 'lecture', 'sleeping' and 'sweeping', 'water' and 'daughter'.

Many poets think of their inspiration as being a female muse. Walcott uses this notion to meditate on the juxtaposition of beauty and ugliness, the power of beauty to dispel ugliness (for a while), the relative values of merchandising goods and words, the rise and fall of cultures, and the survival of artefacts when their creators have long ceased to be.

Castiliane: place-name, deriving ultimately from Latin 'castellanum', governor of a castle. The European explorers often established fortified castles to guard their trade routes. The phrase 'castles in Spain' is an idiom for 'daydreams'

GOLONDRINA: Spanish for the 'swallow', a songbird

Creole architecture: architecture which developed in the New World, often blending different styles

asterisk: Walcott often uses metaphors that are drawn from language. In 'Chapter X' of 'Tales of the Islands', he compares the foam on the shore to handwriting. Here, he compares the wrought-iron flowers to the star-shaped character *. This same character is often used in scholarly works to indicate a footnote. This meaning ties in with Walcott's notion that someone might use pictures of the wrought-iron to illustrate a lecture

apertures: openings

wraith: an apparition of a person who once lived. Its appearance is often linked to a death. Is it the death of a culture here?

noon's despair: the time when the sun is at its height and when there are no shadows. Since there are no real shadows, the poet creates his own

Donna: a gift. 'Donna' is a term of respect for a female in Italian. It comes from 'domina', 'lady'

grace: Walcott often uses words which have religious connotations. We have 'redeemed' in stanza 1, 'grace' here and 'sign' in stanza 3. 'Grace' has several meanings, including, elegant movement, a pleasing quality, a favour

muslin: fine material. The word comes from Arabic and is one of the links in the poem between the Spanish and their Moorish conquerors

black duennas: female chaperones wearing black clothes. Duennas were often widowed relatives

bandol: band. A Spanish 'bandurria' was a stringed instrument like a lute

molasses: treacle

stevedores: men who load and unload ships

faun: a figure in Roman mythology, part man and part animal

fin de siècle: end of century. The phrase is often applied to the end of the nineteenth century. It suggested weariness, satiation and decadence

Alhambras: the original 'Alhambra' was a fortified palace built by the Moors in Granada, Spain, during the thirteenth and fourteenth centuries, a time when Islam was well established in Spain. In Britain, the name was subsequently applied to ornate dance halls. Walcott suggests a parallel between the Moorish invasion of Spain and the Spanish invasion of the Caribbean

coign: more usually spelt 'quoin', a cornerstone

da Falla: Manuel de Falla (1876–1946) was a Spanish composer, best known for his music for the bullring

assignation: lovers' meeting

bells: church bells, perhaps

male, malodorous sea: the sea is normally described as female, partly because its gender is feminine in most European languages. Walcott associates it with sailors and merchants and stevedores, suggesting that it partakes of their characteristics

cheap enamel wares: there is more money in transporting cheap goods than in writing poetry

Doña Maria: respectful title; Maria is a very common name in Spain. Perhaps Walcott is moving from 'frail Donna' to 'Doña Maria', the quintessential Spanish woman

'A Lesson for this Sunday'

SUMMARY:
I lie in my hammock on a warm Sunday morning. There is nothing to disturb my idleness as I look at the butterflies, listen to the maid's song, sip lemonade and swing. Two small children begin to chase the butterflies, catching one and partially disembowelling it, before the maid takes them away. The peace of mind is gone. Cruelty is endemic in the living. Even the grass grows to be cut down.

COMMENTARY AND NOTES:
The poem's title suggests a religious message and we are provided with a message, although it is not a comfortable one. It is a Darwinian message suggesting that Nature is 'red in tooth and claw', and that human beings, even apparently innocent children, are part of the cycle of cruelty. The poem is highly patterned, with rhymes and words being repeated to mimic the repetition of cruelty. The vocabulary has strong religious connotations, seen in 'lesson', 'Sunday', 'rituals', 'protestant hosanna' 'sabbath', 'sin', 'prays' and 'sign', and there is a covert comparison between the 'frail', 'yellow'-winged butterfly and the 'frail' girl in a 'lemon' frock.

the lemonade of simple praise: this parallels the well-known phrase 'the milk of human kindness'

lepidopterists: people who study moths and butterflies

mantis: usually a 'praying mantis', a green carnivorous insect which rests with its front legs raised as if in prayer. There is a possible pun in 'prays', suggesting 'preys'

The mind swings: the mind can no longer avoid thought as in the first stanza, where only the hammock swings

And everywhere ... torn: this line is very similar to one of Yeats's in 'The Second Coming' (1921), 'And everywhere the ceremony of innocence is drowned', where Yeats uses religious language to create his vision of the present and future

'Allegre'

SUMMARY:
Some mornings seem to be as alive and excited as pigeons flying to a known destination and clutching eagerly at the branch on which they alight. This morning is full of blue smoke and the promise of richness, from the honey of wild bees, and the prospect of adventure for young boys. Everything in nature seems neat and orderly, and the human mind seems to reflect this peaceful harmony. Men are cutting trees to make into dugout canoes. There are none of the trappings of urban civilisation, just

natural beauty. Finding one's own identity and knowing one's roots is not easy and may not bring happiness. Perhaps it is significant that the sky can appear most beautiful in a drought, when it presages suffering.

COMMENTARY AND NOTES:
This poem starts in elation and ends in meditation. In the ecstatic, romantic opening, there is no end rhyme, just the rhythms of excited speech and the internal harmonies of alliteration ('crossing', 'slopes', 'silver', 'sunlight', 'sides', 'singer'), assonance ('sunlight', 'white', 'sides', 'delight', 'prime') and repetition ('and' four times, 'blue' three times, 'sun' in 'sunlight' twice, 'sunward', 'sunrise'). As thoughtfulness replaces spontaneity, the lines tend to end with punctuation marks, the metre becomes more regular and rhyme appears, obviously linking 'sea', 'identity', 'Italy' and 'empty', and more subtly chiming 'ridges' and 'hillsides', 'sunlight' and 'drought'.

Allegre:	French for 'cheerful', 'lighthearted', 'happy'
Silver . . . range:	the pigeons seem to change colour depending on their background
lignum-vitae:	wood of life, tropical trees with blue and purple flowers. In some Catholic ceremonies on Good Friday, the cross is held high and the priest sings 'Lignum Christi' – this is the cross of Christ on which hung the Saviour of the world
As the . . . prime:	as a singer gets older, his lower notes tend to get stronger and more mellow
wild bees and briersmoke:	a traditional way to retrieve wild honey is to blow smoke into the hive. The smoke does not hurt the bees but it makes them drowsy and allows the hunters to take away the honey
wind-honed:	shaped and straightened by the wind
diligence:	careful attention
campeche:	type of tree probably native to Mexico, easy to carve
gommiers:	gum trees
ewer:	large jug, water carrier. Walcott ironically refers to the sky that presages drought as a 'ewer'

'Conqueror'

SUMMARY:
This poem invites the reader to contemplate a figure of destruction almost as if it were a painting or a carving. The conqueror who has inculcated discipline, if not valour, in his armies has stopped on the top of a hill. His gloved hands are on the front of his saddle, his eyes show little emotion. He is mighty and in his destructiveness seems only part human. He can

almost envy the weak humanity of his victims, but his weakness is held in and circumscribed by his armour. Below him, in the rain, he can pick out the crops, the flocks, a herder and a rider passing through a river and between poplars. On the distant hills, it may be snowing and everything he can see is experiencing the kind of peace that often precedes a storm. They are like the sparrows that fly about, unaware of the destruction that is to be unleashed. The birds can be interpreted as symbols of innocence which trust in God, or representatives of thought which can switch from one place of rest to another. Perhaps, if one of them cried out, the conqueror might be moved to pity, or he might raise his hand to signal the onslaught on the valley below.

COMMENTARY AND NOTES:
In 'Conqueror', the poet tries to make the sound echo the sense. The opening stanza contains a high proportion of the 'b', 'p', 'd', 'g' and 'k' sounds. These are explosive sounds, hard and of short duration, are evocative of the sounds of war and of hooves on hard rock. The final stanza also contains these sounds, but the punctuation cuts the lines into shorter units, indicating a sense of urgency and impatience.

The poem is in five stanzas of unequal length; the metre varies to reflect the meaning; and the rhyme scheme is highly patterned, as inescapable as the conqueror. Notice, for example, that an important word in one stanza, for example 'hour' in line 7, is picked up in 'devour' in stanza 3 and in 'power' in the final stanza. The hour of the conqueror has come and his power is invincible.

As one would expect in a poem with such a title, there is a vocabulary of violence: 'flayer', 'armies', 'scaled', 'dragonish', 'furies', 'victim', 'armour', 'cages', 'slaughter', 'murderous', 'devour', 'claws', 'torturer', 'conqueror' and 'desolation'. What is less expected but equally striking is the vocabulary that has religious connotations: 'light', 'deliverer', 'deity', 'victim', 'flocks', 'peace', 'sparrows', 'glory', 'mass', 'innocence', 'pity', 'god' and 'respite'. Just as we found cruelty and innocence in the children in 'A Lesson for this Sunday', so we find metaphors of peace and destruction here.

pommels:	raised front part of a saddle
dragonish:	in Christian mythology, the devil is often depicted as a dragon. In calling the sky 'dragonish', Walcott is covertly equating inanimate nature and humanity
Iron deliverer:	there are two meanings here, depending on whether we interpret 'iron' as a noun or an adjective. The conqueror may be a deliverer of iron (as in 'gun merchant', a merchant who deals in guns) or a strong deliverer (as in 'the Iron Duke', 'the Iron Lady')

the furies:	the three furies of classical mythology were snake-headed goddesses who pursued unpunished criminals
ravening:	voracious, predatory. In the New Testament, false prophets are described as 'ravening wolves' in 'sheep's clothing' (Matthew 7:15)
whose ... depose:	his armour hides human weaknesses that no amount of murder can dislodge
poplars:	these trees are common in temperate regions
amber landscapes:	the phrase suggests the colour of a painting which has been varnished. The landscape might also be 'amber' because the sun is not very strong
champ:	munch noisily like a horse
spent beyond trembling:	worn out, so exhausted that it can no longer tremble
sparrows:	in the New Testament, Christ told his followers that God was aware of every sparrow (Luke 12:6–7)
pennons:	long flags which taper at the end
iron sheaves:	arrows in a quiver or bundles of spears
And joy ... more:	the thought of lost joys would make the present suffering even less acceptable
sounding brass:	resonant instruments. This phrase is taken from St Paul's epistle to the Corinthians (1 Corinthians 13:1): 'Though I speak with the tongues of men and of angels, and have not charity, I am become as sounding brass, or a tinkling cymbal'

The Castaway

'The Castaway'

SUMMARY:
This poem recreates the thoughts and actions of a person isolated from others. Eyes that have not looked at another human being since the shipwreck, search the sea for any sign of a sail. The empty horizon is endless. Too much activity can cause fear and hysteria in case I mistake my own footprints for those of someone else. I lie quietly, watching the apparently motiveless actions of wind and wave, looking at the flowers and the futile movement of sandflies. My quiet activities are those of an old man, thinking as I empty myself and my mind. Excrement, bleaching in the sun, seems to become part of the elements, just like humans, who were made from dust, and return to dust. In the silence, I can hear the coral reef grow, and the noise of killing a louse is like thunder. I am totally in control, seemingly divine, but gradually being destroyed and losing the

sense of being immortal. The brain creates corruption in very much the same way as an over-ripe fruit can be a breeding-ground for insects, and in my desolation I am perhaps more like the suffering god on the cross than the all-seeing god of power.

COMMENTARY AND NOTES:
This poem, composed entirely of short stanzas, is a montage of images and apparently unconnected ideas. However, there is a subtle undercurrent of rhyme, clearly connecting 'lie' and 'multiply', 'man', 'plan' and 'began', 'art' and 'heart', and 'sand' and 'hand', and less overtly linking 'morsel' and 'sail', 'child' and 'filled', and 'nothing', 'considering', 'hatching'. The castaway speaks in the first person, but we learn little about him, except some of the effects of loneliness and isolation. He is at one and the same time totally in control and totally helpless.

The vocabulary is unpleasant, beginning with 'starved', continuing with 'afraid', emphasising boredom and tiredness, the sense of nothingness, the waste of life represented by body waste, 'evacuation' and 'faeces', the infestation of 'sandflies', 'sea-lice' and 'maggots', the 'choked' bottle and the 'nailed' hand.

The poem is meant to dispel the romantic associations many of us have about living on a desert island. This castaway is tortured by loneliness.

starved:	the metaphor of starvation is carried on as the castaway seeks even a 'morsel' of a sail
threads:	leads it on. There is a pun here. The horizon is like an infinite thread in the eye of a needle
Sailing . . . palm:	sailing in my imagination, the shadow making me think of the ripples a ship makes as it moves through the sea
lest:	in case
nothing:	no matter how hard he looks, he sees nothing, except things that he would never see if he had company
evacuation:	emptying
entrails:	intestines, internal organs
genesis:	in the Book of Genesis, Adam was made 'of the dust of the ground' (Genesis 2:7)
polyp:	coral is built up over centuries from the shells and skeletons of marine organisms, 'polyps'
thwanged:	Walcott gives us this example of onomatopœia to describe the effect of the sound of two waves crashing together
Godlike:	resembling a god
godhead:	the essential nature of god
babel:	a play on 'babble', a confusion of noises and voices. In the Old Testament, men built the Tower of Babel

gospel: (that is, Gate to God) so that they would never again die in a Deluge. God changed their languages so that they could not understand each other (Genesis 11:9) good news. The bottle contains sand rather than a human message

Clenched ... hand: the bottle indicates that there has been a shipwreck and, if so, the ship is clenched tight on the floor of the sea, fastened there as if by nails and washed clean. The image here is of the crucifixion

'The Swamp'

SUMMARY:

A swamp is permanently waterlogged. It is usually overgrown with trees and shrubs. This one is seen as a living entity, spreading and deadly, although superficially attractive. It is alive and growing, frightening even to the brave. Negro slaves often tried to escape into the swamps, often to die there. The mangrove trees intertwine like serpents, frightening and unnatural, hiding animals, flowers and insects and worrying the travellers who try to cross the swamp. The darkness is like sleep or like death, something we cannot control.

COMMENTARY AND NOTES:

This poem of 33 lines is made up of 11 stanzas, each of three lines, except for stanza 1 (two lines) and stanza 3 (four lines). The metre is irregular, mirroring the seemingly unpatterned thoughts expressed, but rhymes abound. We find half-rhyme in 'mouth' and 'growth', 'rot' and 'root'; eye rhyme in 'mood' and 'blood', 'bed' and 'rooted'; and full rhyme in 'shallows' and 'Negroes', 'toad' and 'road', 'death' and 'breath'. Nor is the rhyme limited to the end of lines. Internal rhyme links 'clear' and 'smear', 'deep' and 'sleep', 'backward' and 'black'. The repeated sounds reinforce the repeated images of growth, procreation and death. And rhyme is not the only repeated sound pattern. Limiting ourselves to the first 12 lines, we find assonance in 'hums' and 'fungi', 'sun' 'gully' and 'blood'; and hard explosive alliteration in 'black', 'behind', 'bed' and 'blood'; and in 'come', 'canebreak', 'quarry', 'clear', 'cracker' and 'convicts'. The first image is of eating with 'Gnawing' and 'mouth'. The animal image is reinforced by 'viscous breath', 'blood' and 'serpentlike'. Sexual images clearly occur with 'vulva' and 'phalloi', and these are reinforced throughout the last section of the poem.

Hums: there is a great deal of insect life in a swamp. Insects may be responsible for the onomatopœic 'hum'

viscous: thick and sticky. This adjective is usually applied to liquids

mottling:	streaking
canebreak:	a thicket of sugarcane, almost impenetrable
quarry:	an open mine for extracting rock. There is a possible pun in that a quarry is also an animal or bird that is tracked and hunted

sun-shocked gully-bed: dried-out water channel. Dogs can be put off the scent by water. If there is no water, the dogs usually catch their quarry

Hemingway's hero: Ernest Hemingway (1899–1961) often wrote about macho heroes. One of his heroes, Nick, in 'Two-Hearted River' (1925), did not want to venture into a swamp

Limbo:	an intermediate place, neither heaven nor hell
cracker convicts:	first-class criminals, excellent at finding a means of escape
smear:	at sunset, the mosquitoes begin to bite, sucking the blood of anyone in the swamp
sinuosities:	lithe, thin, curved shapes
mangrove:	tropical evergreen tree or shrub. It has stilt-like, intertwining roots.
clutch:	(1) grasp; (2) nest of eggs
ginger-lily:	plant with reddish-brown petals
vulva:	external female genitals. The bell-like opening of the tiger-orchid is being compared to the vulva. Only certain insects can pollinate it
phalloi:	relating to the male genitals
decrescence:	diminishing, waning
fast-filling:	rapidly darkening. In the tropics, night comes suddenly. There is rarely more than 30 minutes between daylight and darkness
last ... throat:	the bird drinking water just before nightfall seems to be drinking darkness
amnesia:	loss of memory
chaos:	utter confusion, the formlessness that existed before the universe came into being

---

'The Flock'

SUMMARY:
Winter is becoming established and the last of the migratory birds begin to head south. They are heading for the warmth and light of the tropics, while I awoke this morning to increased cold but also to a wealth of images flying through the mind. In my mind's eye, I see a knight on horseback, infinitesimally small against the snow-covered mountain, bravely pursuing

his objective. I, too, am journeying alone and in silence, using words on paper to act out the impulses of my mind. The world has moved through the seasons since the beginning of time, while people, languages and climatic ages have come and gone. The Arctic behaves as it has always done, impartially, unaware of the mastodons it has buried, or the seals that howl on its surface, or the birds that fly over it. May the human mind also show its constancy as long as it exists, and may it always welcome visiting thoughts as I welcomed the migration that inspired this poem.

COMMENTARY AND NOTES:

The title 'The Flock' might make us think of sheep, rather than of the subject of the poem: migration, winter, the passage of time, the beauty of courage and stoicism, and the value of nature to the poet. The poem is in three verse paragraphs of 22, 16 and 10 lines. The description 'verse paragraphs' is used because this is the first poem we have looked at where new lines do not begin with a capital letter unless they are beginning a new sentence. Yet this is not 'free verse' in an absolute sense, because rhyme holds the verse together in the same way as arctic ice controls the water and the land. In keeping with the meaning, the rhyme is most apparent in the first section; it becomes less so in the second section as the poet muses; and it disappears as the poet finds consolation in thoughts of human endurance and in their ability to emulate the birds' response to instinct.

The main images in the poem are of a flock of birds moving across the sky as if they have been shot from a bow; the knight, silhouetted against an alpine mountain, struggling through the snow; the poet making marks on paper; the regular revolutions of the earth; the obduracy of the Arctic; and the strength and balance of the mind, finding its blessings in such things as birds flying to the warmth.

teal and mallard: migratory ducks
longbows: powerful medieval hand-held bows
Skeletal forest: the tundra is often defined as the region between the Poles and the timberline, i.e. the region where trees can grow. There are only a few trees here, so the knight is far north
sepulchral: gloomy, tomblike, associated with death
tarn: small mountain lake
cannonading: bombarding
Vizor'd: (1) covered with a visor, a piece of armour which protects the face; (2) wearing a peaked cap
augury: the art of interpreting signs and omens
prepossession: favourable bias; advance ownership
larks: (1) songbirds; (2) pranks
mastodon: extinct elephant-like animal. Its skeleton has been found in glaciers

tundras:	vast frozen areas between the North Pole and the zone where trees can survive
annihilation:	extinction
fixity:	unchanging quality, inflexibility, the ability to endure a situation
equinox:	periods in the temperate zones when day and night both last 12 hours, usually March 21 and September 21

'The Whale, His Bulwark'

SUMMARY:
Praising the magnitude of a whale may provoke a hostile reaction because it is now unfashionable to write paeans, or poems of joy. Formerly, the whale was admired; formerly whalers harpooned whales, causing great suffering. On one occasion, I heard of a whale that was beached and cut up for food by islanders. The boy who told me the story had seen it but could hardly believe what he saw. I believe that he told me the truth. When I was a child, one could believe in God, and whales could beach themselves on the shore. Whales are much less common now, and God is just as invisible as ever. Yet I'm grateful to God that I can praise things that I don't understand, that I haven't lost my sense of awe, even if awe is unfashionable now.

COMMENTARY AND NOTES:
This is one of the simplest of Walcott's poems, simple in form and meaning. It comes from a sequence of poems 'A Tropical Bestiary', which contains 'Ibis', 'Octopus', 'Lizard', 'Man O' War Bird', 'Sea Crab' and 'Tarpon' as well as 'The Whale, His Bulwark'. Walcott compares the whale, the poet and God, all capable of inspiring awe, all undervalued in our society. There is a tendency to use repetition in twos and threes: we have 'To praise' and 'To write', 'believe' and 'believed'; we also have three stanzas, three entities being humbled, three uses of 'once'.

The prevailing tone is of controlled sadness and distaste. The control is shown in the density of rhymes ('jet' and 'yet', 'curse' and 'verse', 'eyes', 'prize' and 'size', 'mythological', 'small' and 'apocryphal', and 'possible', 'unfathomable' and 'unfashionable'); in the alliteration (notice, for example, the words beginning with 'b' and 'g'); and in the assonance ('praise', 'whale' and 'baleine'). The distaste is shown in the choice of unpleasant words ('curse', 'humbled', 'threshed', 'derisive', 'antlike', 'pygmy', 'dead', 'foundered' and 'unfashionable').

His Bulwark:	God's defence. In the Old Testament, God's messenger, Jonah, was swallowed by a whale and thus saved from drowning

bulwark:	fortification, defence against injury, breakwater, a structure along the outward sides of the deck
The high . . . yet:	this resembles the refrain often found in Old English elegiac poetry: 'How the mighty are fallen!'
those . . . verse:	those who have no respect for God, the animal kingdom or the power of poetry
threshed:	beat the water, tossed and turned. Notice that 'thresh' is used instead of 'thrash', giving the added connotation of the whale as a harvester figure
baleine:	French for 'whale'
Grenadines:	a chain of about 600 small islands in the Caribbean. They are part of the Windward Islands
fleshed:	the verb 'to flesh' has several meanings: (1) to incite animals to hunt by giving them small pieces of flesh; (2) to wound the flesh with a weapon; (3) to incite to bloodshed; (4) to remove the flesh; (5) to fatten
antlike:	compared with the whale, the villagers were 'antlike' in size and in activity, seemingly rushing about aimlessly
Salt-crusted:	covered with salt from the sea, but also covered with salt to preserve the meat
mythological:	amazing, something from a folk story
couldn't . . . eyes:	was so surprised that he could hardly believe what he was seeing. 'Believe' is used with different meanings in adjacent lines, just as 'fleshed' is used with deliberate ambiguity above
foundered:	sunken, collapsed
I praise the unfathomable:	this direct expression of his opinion reminds us of a similar interposition in 'Byzantium' (1930) by W. B. Yeats: 'I hail the superhuman;/I call it death-in-life and life-in-death'
unfathomable:	incapable of being understood, incomprehensible; particularly appropriate as it derives from fathom, a measurement of sea depth
Though . . . dead:	this phrase is again deliberately ambiguous. It may mean that the boy who told him the story may be dead or that the boy in himself (that is, his youthful innocence and idealism) may be dead
apocryphal:	of questionable authenticity

'Missing the Sea'

SUMMARY:
When we are used to a steady, regular sound, and it is suddenly removed,

we notice the silence. We are aware that something is wrong, but we cannot be certain what it is. The loss of such a sound is like a blow that leaves our senses reeling. The silence seems to surround the valley, to weigh on the mountains, to make the familiar seem unfamiliar, to inspire a poem. It seems to make all the other senses more acute: we see more clearly; we notice smells. We are aware of it, as we are aware of the loss of a loved one, that we long to have back again.

COMMENTARY AND NOTES:
The imagery in this poem is reinforced by the language: nothing is quite right. The curtains hang lifeless; the mirror does not reflect properly; the valley is held in by a hoop of silence; the mountain is weighed down by it. The language too is not quite right: 'weighs this mountain' would normally mean 'takes the weight of this mountain', rather than 'weighs heavily on the mountain'; normally people, not gestures, are 'estranged'; we expect 'a thick' thing, not 'a thick nothing'; and the dead cannot 'behave', although, in our minds, we can make them behave in a way that suits us. Language and imagery conspire to create a sense of unnatural loss.

Missing the Sea: the title, at first, seems clear. The speaker is used to the sea and feels nostalgic for it, almost saying, 'I am missing the sea'. Later, we might wonder if the title does not also suggest that the sea is absent: 'Missing: the sea'

drapes: curtains
stuns: renders unconscious, dazed
hoops: encircles
pushes this pencil: makes me write
Freights: weighs down
sour laundry: damp washing that has not been hung out to dry and so lacks the smell of air-dried clothes
As ... beloved: when people that we love die, we do not want to change things. We want to stop time for ourselves, just as time has stopped for the people who have died
expecting occupancy: the dead person is like a room which is prepared and ready to be occupied. The exterior is there, but the spirit missing

'The Glory Trumpeter'

SUMMARY:
Old Eddie's face told much about his life and his life-style. He could play his trumpet to suit all tastes, traditional and modern. When he stood up to play, I thought of the past, of my grandmother's home, about reading

comics on a Sunday, about people who had gone to the United States. If Eddie's face told the story of what we might become, I did not know it when I was a child and saw the men who returned from the United States, men changed in accent, appearance and demeanour. Eddie turned to face the sea, to face the cities of America, and the music made me feel guilty for all those who suffered because of their race or because they were away from their loved ones. I shared the race and some of the feelings of exile were self-imposed.

COMMENTARY AND NOTES:
This poem deals with the problems of inheriting two cultures and yet belonging fully to neither. The poet, like Eddie, may turn his back on the West Indies and on the young who are more interested in 'swilling liquor' than in listening, but Galveston and Mobile cannot hear him either. 'The Glory Trumpeter' has four stanzas of 10, 11, 9 and 10 lines. The metre is regular, a fitting counterpoint to the meditative nature of the theme, and Walcott makes considerable use of rhyme ('lights' and 'nights', 'meted' and 'defeated'), alliteration (notice the pattern of 'l's and 'r's in stanza 1), and assonance (especially the short 'i' sounds in 'Mississippi', 'swivelling' and 'indifference').

Two of the most noticeable features of the poem are the use of vocabulary associated with black culture ('jesus-ragtime', 'gut-bucket blues') and the playing with several levels of meaning. Eddie's trumpet is compared with Joshua's horn, with the Cornucopia, the horn of plenty that America seemed to poor West Indians; and the Gulf of Mexico is a symbol of the gulf between the poet and the people he is leaving, and between him and the people in America, represented by the uncle that he will never contact.

The Glory Trumpeter: the juxtaposition is unusual. It may refer to the angels on the last day who will blow their trumpet to announce the glory of the Second Coming. The word 'glory' has many meanings, including exaltation, praise, honour, adoration and the beauty and bliss of heaven

Mississippi: the second-longest river in the United States
avuncular: friendly, helpful, like an uncle
wakes: vigils or celebrations at the time of a death
cathouse: slang for 'brothel'
'Georgia ... Saves': popular song or hymn
sealed: closed so tightly as to be almost blind
deacon: official in the church
barracks: housing for military or police, building used to house people temporarily
sallow: of sickly complexion

wharves:	landing platforms at a harbour
jesus-ragtime:	style of jazz with elements of negro spirituals
gut-bucket blues:	highly emotional style of playing
funereal serge:	dark, cheap, heavy clothes; the colours like those worn at a funeral
homburgs:	soft felt hats with stiff upturned brims
Joshua:	Old Testament leader who ordered his priests to blow their ram's horn trumpets continuously for seven days, and then commanded the Israelites to shout, so causing the walls of Jericho to fall (Joshua 6:1–20). The story of Joshua is told in a number of negro spirituals, including 'Joshua at the Battle of Jericho'
Gulf:	Gulf of Mexico

Mobile and Galveston: cities in Alabama and Texas on the Gulf of Mexico. Both cities are associated with the oil business

---

'Laventille'

SUMMARY:

The slum huddled precariously at the top of the hill, much higher than the better suburbs down nearer the city. We climbed up to Laventille, where the children of former slaves lived in crowded squalor. The structure of society was reflected in the stratified nature of the hill: the higher up the hill, the lower one's social position. People who were transported as slaves had no idea how they would end, and the suffering has not disappeared. The legacy of slavery is one of the gifts to be passed on to the child who is about to be baptised. The people at the church, dressed in their best attire, aspired to a better quality of life. These were the people I had once loved but was now set apart from. How many of us really want to think about our past as slaves? After the ceremony, photographs are taken, carefully so as to avoid including the headstones in the churchyard, and polite words are spoken. Looking down, towards the city, I feel saddened and apart from the others. We left in Africa a way of life that we never found again. Slavery hurt us and we have not totally died to the old world of Africa nor been totally born to the new world in the Caribbean.

COMMENTARY AND NOTES:

This is a strongly felt poem, in which Walcott discusses the traumas inflicted on Africans who were enslaved, carried to the New World, and who are now caught between two worlds. There is a suggestion that Christianity has not helped very much, merely added a veneer of respectability. A useful exercise with this poem would be to follow four themes: poverty, the baptism, 'the middle passage' and the attitude of the speaker.

Examine them separately first and then see how poverty is linked to the middle passage, and how the poet uses the ceremony of baptism to comment on Christianity. One way of doing this is to make lists of words that are associated with each theme and then to compare them. The 'Episcopal' buzzards link the slums and the church; and the corrugated rooftops are linked with the waves on the journey from Africa.

Alliteration plays a considerable role in the poem. In 1. 13, for example, we have 'gutters growled and gargled', where the hard sound reflects the unpleasant realities of life in a slum. The lines vary in length from one word (1. 7) to ten words (1. 40), suggesting perhaps that some ideas are dwelt on, while others come rushing out. This is reinforced by the run-on lines and the run-on stanzas. The rhyme scheme, too, is irregular, although all-pervasive. It is almost as if the poet is seeking to understand the pattern in the lives of the people he describes.

Laventille:	there are a number of French place-names in Trinidad. 'Laventille' was a shanty town overlooking Port-of-Spain, the capital of Trinidad. It was higher up the mountain than the more affluent suburbs. There is a possible pun in that 'laver' means 'wash' and so the slum is linked with the waters of baptism
V. S. Naipaul:	Trinidadian writer, born in 1932
tinkling:	making a high tinny sound. Trinidad is thought to be the home of steel bands. This line may mean that there was little shelter, but there was, at least, some music
favelas:	hillside slums in Rio de Janeiro, the huge city in Brazil that used to be its capital
Episcopal:	bishop-like
turkey-buzzards:	an American vulture which has dark plumage and a reddish-purple head. Bishops sometimes wear purple birettas (square caps) as a mark of their rank
Belmont ... St Clair:	middle-class suburbs of Port-of-Spain
water catchment:	area bounded by watersheds, i.e. a wet area
carousel:	a merry-go-round
hovels:	ramshackle dwellings
the middle passage:	the long journey across the Atlantic from West Africa to the West Indies made by slaves. The conditions on the ships were appalling. Space and food were inadequate; the African slaves were often kept manacled in the hold; and, if there was bad weather, they were often thrown overboard, to reduce the weight of the cargo
hatch:	'under hatch' is the nautical equivalent of 'below deck', 'out of sight'

felonies:	serious crimes, like arson and murder
breadfruit:	fruit of a tree that is native to the Pacific islands but transported to the West Indies as cheap nutrition for slaves
escalated:	terraced, in steps as on an escalator
corrugated:	in ridges and troughs, like the waves of the sea
annex:	extension to a main building
talc:	soft mineral found in rocks, talcum powder
verger:	a church official who often acts as a caretaker
akimbo:	this word usually means with hands on hips and elbows stuck out. It originally meant 'in a keen bow', that is, sharply curved
Godfather:	(1) God the father; (2) godfather, sponsor in baptism
supercilious:	arrogantly contemptuous
rachitic:	like someone with rickets (that is, with soft bones and bow legs) but also suggesting arthritic
'across . . . life':	quotation from a popular hymn
retching waters:	the sea which makes one vomit, the heaving sea
patient:	long-suffering
habitual wombs:	women who are constantly giving birth, perhaps due to the social pressures on them
cleft:	split open
amnesiac:	something that causes loss of memory
swaddling:	this adjective is normally applied to pieces of cloth used to wrap a new-born baby
cerements:	burial clothes

'The Almond Trees'

SUMMARY:
In the early morning, there is no relic of history here except this group of almond trees and a fisherman throwing a stick for his dog. By midday, there are sun-bathing girls on the beach, their golden-brown bodies making them look like classical nymphs. The heat has turned the trunks of the almond trees (and the skins of the girls) the same colour as the metal understructure of a barge, or of the boats that were used to transport African women to the West Indies. These young women have inherited their colour and their strength from their ancestors who suffered but survived. Old trees are the same colour as sun-tanned limbs. Just as trees were cut down and used for boats, so were the African women culled from their birthplace. Both faced the waves and the sun on the 'middle passage'. Both learned to grow and communicate in a foreign land. The African women were not like hamadryads, who died when the tree died. They cried but they lived. One young woman unconsciously acknowledges the

relationship between the African women and the almond trees, both of which were transported. She moves to lie down under the shade of the trees and they, like loving parents, look on in silence.

COMMENTARY AND NOTES:

This poem compares African women and almond trees, both newcomers to the islands, both beautiful and productive, both now living in peace, apparently unaware of their turbulent histories. The fate of African women was a cruel one. Walcott could have offered a strident criticism of the way they were treated. Instead, he shows their beauty, their strength, their ability to survive in spite of their suffering.

The poem is extremely well organised, with the physical attributes of the trees being grafted on to those of the women. There is freedom in the length of line and the number of lines per stanza, but there is tight control of the ideas, the vocabulary, the rhyme and the rhythm.

almond:	a tree with pink flowers and green fruit containing a light-brown edible seed
stand:	a group of trees in a particular area, often planted deliberately close together
sea-almond:	almond trees that flourish near the sea
no visible history:	the earliest human beings left no visible tracks on the earth: no buildings, no records. It was almost as if they had never existed
this . . . Africa:	because so many Africans were transported to the Caribbean, the island shores are like an outpost of Africa
forked limbs:	Shakespeare, in *King Lear* (*c.* 1605), described man as 'a poor, bare, forked animal'
Pompeian bikinis:	in AD79, Vesuvius erupted, killing many of the inhabitants of Pompeii. Many were covered in lava while performing everyday activities and their shapes were preserved. The image suggests the brevity of life, the uncertainty of the future. It also refers to the well-preserved Pompeian friezes, in some of which there were women who looked as if they were wearing bikinis
daphnes:	Daphne was a nymph in Greek mythology. She was transformed into a laurel tree to preserve her from being raped by Apollo. The reference to Afro-Caribbean women being 'brown daphnes' suggests that they, too, have been chased and raped. This is also linked to 'forked limbs', where the women's legs are covertly compared with the branches of trees

sacred grove:	laurel groves were sacred in Greek and Roman traditions. A laurel wreath was placed on one's head as a sign of honour
frieze:	decorated section of wall. Many friezes were found intact, when Pompeii was excavated
acetylene:	a colourless gas capable of reaching very high temperatures and used to cut and weld metals. The warm tropical air bronzes the bodies like an acetylene torch
aged limbs:	the young women are the descendants of others who have suffered and survived. If we can have 'an ancient people', then we can have 'aged limbs'
cured:	healed, preserved
furnace:	the fierce fires of life. In the Old Testament (Daniel 3:6–30), three of Daniel's companions, Shadrach, Meshach and Abednego, were put into a fiery furnace by King Nebuchadnezzar. They were miraculously preserved from the fire
broad dialect:	a variety of language. The rustling of the leaves is like a form of speech
hamadryad:	in classical mythology, a nymph that lives in a tree and dies when the tree dies
boles:	tree trunks, reddish brown pigments
metamorphosis:	complete change of physical form

'Lampfall'

SUMMARY:
A family is often closest in the evenings when the members congregate near the lamp. We are like the group of people in Wright's painting, listening to a lecture on the astrolabe, a device for taking measurements at sea, and being bathed and almost blessed by the light that falls on us. I never weary of the sound of the ocean or of the trees rustling and promising fulfilment. But there's a monster that lurks deep in my subconscious that occasionally causes me to despair. It transports me from the people and places I love, making me think of extinction, an extinction that I might wish for if it weren't for you, my family and friends. All day you've watched the sea, and the daily activities. Love can draw us back from the brink of oblivion. At night, we have listened to the sounds of the forest. We seem to belong here. And we have hope, for the morning star, the symbol of hope, appears. Like you, I preferred nature in its simple state to the technologically advanced society that is symbolised by the motor car.

COMMENTARY AND NOTES:
This poem might well be read in conjunction with Hamlet's 'To be or not

to be' speech. It deals with the attraction of dying, of ceasing to feel pain. The speaker in the poem is held back by the love of family and friends and the realisation that death would also involve loss.

Walcott uses the period of 'lampfall' as a metaphor for the in-between stage between wanting to live and wanting to die. There is considerable attraction in being at one with the primal elements, and some anguish at the present love of technology.

Notice the precise vocabulary ('metaphor', 'astrological', 'benediction'), drawn from language, science and religion. There is also a set of words associated with fishing and this overlaps with the religious set. Notice also the tendency to link the separate stanzas by a pattern of rhymes: 'quarrelling' in 1 with 'barrelling' in 2, 'heard' in 5 with 'preferred' in 6, and the support given to such linkage by half-rhyme ('edge' and 'aged', 'eyes' and 'gaze'), alliteration (e.g. 'green, glaucous gaze') and assonance (especially the long 'ee' sounds in 'sea's', 'leaves', 'me', 'see', 'green' and 'beetles').

lampfall: this word is a coinage, based on such nouns as 'landfall' (sighting land when one is at sea) and 'nightfall' (the coming of night). The more usual compound with 'lamp' is 'lamplight'

moth-flame metaphor: this refers to the phrase 'like a moth to a flame', meaning what attracts can also be deadly. Unusually for a poet of Walcott's precision, his choice of words here is incorrect as this is a simile, not a metaphor

Coleman: a lamp which burns pressurised fuel, causing a humming noise

Joseph Wright: Joseph Wright of Derby (1734–97) was an artist who painted a picture of a lecture on the astrolabe

'Rejoice, rejoice': words which appear in a carol, 'O come, O come, Emmanuel'

primal fiction: earliest fiction. Many of the earliest stories deal with monsters or serpents, perhaps representative of the latent monster in ourselves

barrelling: travelling very fast

hooked: in both the traditional sense of 'caught like a fish' and in the modern sense of 'addicted'

trolling: (1) a play on 'trawling', in fishing, drawing bait through the water; (2) in Scandinavian folk traditions, trolls were supernatural beings who often lived in caves

plankton: simple organisms inhabiting the surface regions of lakes and seas

phosphorescent: luminescent, related to the emission of light in a chemical reaction. Phosphorus can appear to burn

	when it is immersed in water. 'Phosphorus' is one name for the planet Venus
glaucous:	bluish-green, covered with a waxy film
Penelope:	in Greek mythology, Penelope was the faithful wife of Odysseus. She is sometimes depicted weaving cloth as she waits for her husband to return
Venus:	the second planet from the sun in the solar system, known as the 'morning star' because of its brightness, and also sometimes referred to as 'Phosphorus'
you:	this 'you' may refer to the family and friends, addressed in stanza 3, or to someone else, perhaps another poet who has committed suicide
mining:	miners wear lamps when they go underground. Walcott sees the firefly's light as a lamp, linking it with both the miner and with the group sitting in lamplight
beetles:	cars in general here, but specifically early Volkswagen cars, called 'beetles' because of their shape

The Gulf

'Ebb'

SUMMARY:
Throughout the year and the years, we'll watch our environment being spoiled by industrial waste. Occasionally, we find some natural beauty surviving, but the tractors are ready to move in. We'll see that beauty destroyed too, but we can enjoy it for the moment, and as we enjoy walking in the shade, we can watch imaginary schooners, apparently trapped but capable of setting themselves free. The 'vision' disappears and we are doomed to leave the untouched wilderness. The schooner was part of my childhood which is now long gone. Sometimes still, I see the schooner, or the moon, still glorious, but less so than in the past. Each evening, we all feel a little frightened and this is understandable. From the car in which I travel, I can see enough to be terrified of, and I can see the miraculous in things that I take for granted. Sure . . .

COMMENTARY AND NOTES:
This poem shares some of the feelings expressed by Wordsworth in his sonnet 'The world is too much with us'. Wordsworth felt that we waste what we have and fail to appreciate the beauties of nature:

The sea that bares her bosom to the moon;
The winds that will be howling at all hours,

And are upgathered now like sleeping flowers;
For this, for everything, we are out of tune . . .

Walcott, too, worries that, in the words of the Joni Mitchell song, popular around the time this poem was written: 'They see paradise and they put up a parking lot.'

The poem is made up of 13 three-lined stanzas which are irregular in metre and in their rhyme scheme. In this they mimic the ebb tide. Each time the water comes in, it is almost the same: it makes similar but not identical patterns, and it is a little further out each time until, like the poem, it seems to stop. The punctuation provides us with clues towards interpretation. The first full stop comes after 12 lines in which Walcott presents a picture of our abuse of the environment. The next 12 lines are an almost breathless evocation of the joy there used to be in nature. The lines run on, hurrying to recapture a lost state. In each of these sections, there is only one sentence. In the third section, there are six sentences and the beginnings of a seventh. The stanzas and the lines in this section are compartmentalised, like our adult lives.

Walcott plays with words and structures, insisting on the reader's working in order to unravel his meaning. He uses parallel structures in the last two lines to argue that we can be frightened of things we have regular dealings with, and at the same time marvel at things that we take for granted. Most poems end with a statement; a few end with a question; this one ends with an unfinished comment which is capable of several interpretations. It could be a facile response to Walcott's ideas; it could be an assertion of their validity; it could be a wish to assert their validity. Ironically, when we say 'sure' as in 'I'm sure everything will be all right', we are often doubtful.

Ebb:	the title may be either a noun or a verb. If it is a verb, it means 'flow back, recede'; if it is a noun, it means the period when the tide flows back. The phrase 'at a low ebb' means to be in a state of physical or mental weakness. All these meanings are implicit in the title
treadmill:	an apparatus in which an animal or a person is used to turn a wheel, a monotonous routine
frayed tide:	the 'untidiness' of the tide is like ragged material
rainbow muck:	petrol can leave multicoloured traces on the sand but eventually mixes with the sand to create sludge
afterbirth:	after the birth of a child, the placenta and other foetal tissue is expelled from the womb. The debris on the shore is like industry's afterbirth
scurf:	dandruff, flaky or scaly matter which sticks to a surface
Caterpillar:	this poem in part laments the industrialisation of the

	world. Significantly, the original meaning of this word (the larvae of butterflies) is now applied to large vehicles like tractors and tanks
swift-wickered:	wickerwork is the arrangement of twigs and shoots, often made of bamboo, in a pattern to form items like furniture. The shadows cast by trees change rapidly, creating a wickerwork effect
schooner:	old sailing vessel with at least two masts
lamed heron:	a bird that has been maimed
oil-crippled gull:	when oil gets into the wing feathers, birds are sometimes incapable of flying
washed-up:	exhausted, no longer useful
sere:	dried up, withered
sunfall:	sunset, but suggesting an unnatural event. Compare this coinage with 'lampfall'

'Hawk'

SUMMARY:

There is movement and noise everywhere. The pitiless hawk flies high. The old men, the drinkers, the musicians have heads full of dreams. The Caribs moved through the Caribbean. Humans are merciless, aren't they, hawk? Over the island, you fly. You are like a Spanish nobleman dancing alone, but carrying a knife. Hawk, all the people here are proud of their Spanish inheritance. Above the people, the hawk flies. It has left the leaves of the tree shaking. Servile people long for the power of their masters. It is our turn to be cruel now. But the hawk flies above, making its rough sounds. Hawks cannot make music.

COMMENTARY AND NOTES:

This poem is the fourth in a sequence called 'Metamorphoses' (metamorphosis = complete change of physical form), the others being 'Moon', 'Serpent' and 'Cat'. It has four stanzas of 10, 10, 8 and 7 lines respectively. Many of the lines have three main stresses: 'your wings like extended hands' but extra stresses are used to vary the rhythm.

Perhaps the most obvious feature of the poem is the use of repetition, particularly the line in which the hawk, as 'gabilan', is addressed twice. It occurs in lines 4, 10 and 21 and with a slight variation in line 16, where the affirmative 'ay' is replaced by the questioning 'eh'. The hawk is addressed twice more as 'gabilan' in lines 25 and 32 and the English word 'hawk(s)' occurs three times, so that the bird, in one form or another, is present throughout the poem. It is clearly a symbol of destruction and is rhymed with 'man' who lacks mercy and with the Yucatan, which inspired man's greed.

The vocabulary includes many words which highlight the cruelty of both bird and man ('tigers', 'talons', 'arrows', 'merciless', 'parang', 'spur', 'whips', 'cries'). The one feature which perhaps makes man superior is his music, a music which is echoed by the rhymes and rhythms of the verse.

Hawk: the monosyllabic title is deliberately unusual. We might expect 'The Hawk' or 'A Hawk' but the one-word title allows it to be a noun and a verb. As a noun, it refers to a bird of prey; as a verb, it means to sell in the street, to make a noise in the throat. The hawk often occurs in West Indian folklore. One of the best-known creole proverbs is of significance here: 'Chicken merry, hawk dey near' (When chickens are enjoying themselves, there is a hawk nearby)

treng-ka-treng: onomatopœic, like 'clinkety-clink'

cuatros: fours

Gabilan: Spanish for 'hawk'. Trinidad (which means Trinity) has known three colonial masters: the Spanish, the French and the British. All three European tongues have left relics in the place-names and the creole of the island

Yucatan: an area in central America, part of Mexico. The region was immortalised in legend. There was supposed to be so much gold in the region that it could be found in all the rivers and lakes

Caribs: the people from whom the Caribbean takes its name. The Caribs may well have displaced the peaceful Arawak people from the islands in the Caribbean until they themselves were replaced by the European colonists and their black slaves

catgut: cord made from the intestines of sheep and other animals and used as strings in musical instruments

ocelot: a brown cat-like animal resembling a jaguar, found in the forests of Central America

Arima: place-name

Sangre Grande: place-name meaning 'great blood'. Places of this name are dedicated to the suffering Christ

grandee: Spanish nobleman

parang: a short knife

mestizos: people of mixed parentage, usually Spanish and American Indian

cedars: sweet-smelling trees

Slaves ... talons: this sentence is ambiguous. It may mean (1) slaves long for the cruelty they receive from their masters.

In other words, they are masochistic and enjoy the pain that is inflicted; or (2) slaves long to have the instruments of torture that their masters have. In other words, they wish to inflict the same sort of pain as has been inflicted on them

talons: claws

Rampanalgas: place-name

'Mass Man'

SUMMARY:

A clerk is dressed like a lion. He is followed by a man whose costume makes him look like a peacock. These costumes are like visible figures of speech because of their artistry, ingenuity and brightness. Various people have entered and everyone is dancing and encouraging others to dance, although a child, dressed like a bat, cries. I am dancing like a felon hanging from a gallows, like a bat hanging upside-down. When the carnival is over, someone will be sorry; someone will have to clean up; and someone will have to write your poems.

COMMENTARY AND NOTES:

This four-stanza poem recreates the music and colour of a Trinidadian carnival, the forerunner and inspiration of the Notting Hill Carnival in London. It is written in standard English but the rhyming of 'dance' with 'radiance' suggests that we should read it with the rhythms and intonation of West Indian English. There is in this poem, as in so much of the writing of Walcott, an awareness of the duality of life. In the middle of the carnival pleasures, a child cries; balancing the music and the dance, we have the image of a man dancing, as if in his death throes on the gallows; in today's pleasure is the knowledge of tomorrow's penitence.

Mass Man: the title can mean (1) carnival masquerader; (2) man who goes to Mass; (3) men who congregate together. In West Indian creole, 'man' can be both singular and plural. The carnival normally takes place on Shrove Tuesday, the day before Lent begins on Ash Wednesday. The word 'carnival' means 'goodbye to meat'. Traditionally, meat was not eaten during the period of Lent

mange: an illness which can cause the loss of hair in certain animals, including cats and dogs

clerk: (1) office worker; (2) earlier form of 'cleric', member of the clergy. He could be 'black' because of his colour or because of the colour of his costume

withholds: keeps back, restrains, holds in

metaphors:	figures of speech
coruscating:	emitting flashes of light
mincing:	walking in an affected manner because of the costumes
barges:	(1) moves like a barge; (2) moves abruptly
like Cleopatra:	queen of Egypt. In Shakespeare's *Antony and Cleopatra* (*c.* 1607), Enobarbus describes the splendour of Cleopatra as she floated down the Nile, in a famous speech that begins with the following lines: 'The barge she sat in, like a burnished throne/Burned on the water. The poop was beaten gold'
making style:	dressing up, putting on airs and graces
gibbet:	wooden gallows
bull-whipped:	(1) beaten with a whip made from rawhide; (2) covered in skin and looking like a bull-whip
metronome:	mechanical device to indicate a precise tempo by producing a clicking sound from a pendulum that swings to a chosen rhythm

penitential morning: Ash Wednesday, the day after the carnival

'Landfall, Grenada'

SUMMARY:
Where you are buried, there is no sound from the hills or the sugar cane. The land seems uninterrupted like the sea, whose majesty you hated. The sea was no magical escape route for you. It was a workplace. You chose your final resting place with quiet efficiency, and you rest among the people who loved you. To many, your death was as uneventful as an entry in a ship's log. You suffered in silence. Teach me to die with such calm courage, such indifference to the insignificant words of others.

COMMENTARY AND NOTES:
This elegy for a friend is one of the simplest of Walcott's mature poems. It is in two verses and deals with the life and death of Robert Head in apparently simple, straightforward language. A second or third reading will show unexpected puns and wit, however, especially in the use of the adjective 'deep' and in the dismissal of elegies within an elegy. The metre, like the meaning, seems straightforward. At first, we are struck by its prose-like cadences. If we look more closely, however, we find internal rhyming ('ocean' and 'motion', 'those' and 'impose'), and the proliferation of the sounds 's' and 'z' mimics the sibilance of the sea. Throughout the poem, the vocabulary and metaphors link the grave and the sea. In death, his friend is 'rigidly anchored'; in life, he 'harboured' in certain hearts.

Landfall:	the sighting of land from a ship
Grenada:	a small island state in the Windward Islands
rigidly anchored:	buried
groundswell:	feeling the sea move strongly. Groundswell is often caused by a distant storm or by the effect of waves in shallow water
canes:	sugar cane is still one of the major crops in Grenada
cumuli:	fluffy, low clouds, caused by rising currents of air
seamless ocean:	lands may be segmented and boundaries marked, but the sea appears to belong to all. There may possibly also be a reference here to the 'seamless garment' worn by Christ, for which the Roman soldiers cast lots
tiered sea:	the waves of the sea can appear to rise and fall like steps
mythology:	collection of stories relating to a particular people or culture
ruled stars:	early mariners often plotted their journeys by using the Pole Star; modern mariners need not be ruled by the stars
your . . . entry:	your death may not have seemed any more momentous than an entry in a ship's log or record book
Deep friend:	(1) very close friend; (2) sailor friend (the sea is often referred to as 'the deep'); (3) buried friend
elegies:	poetic laments for the dead

'Homecoming: Anse La Raye'

SUMMARY:
When we were at school, we learned about the ancient Greeks and about the characters involved in the Trojan war. One thing we did not learn was that people returning 'home' are not always welcomed in the way they expect. The island children, showing signs of malnutrition, think you are a tourist because you are well-dressed and they rush to you asking for money. Once you were a carefree child, too, looking out to sea and running about on the beach. You were not thinking of a career then, but today you'd like them to acknowledge that you are a poet, and their poet. You knew you might not be eulogised as a poet but you hadn't realised that coming to the place of your birth is not the same as coming 'home'. You don't give them any money and they go off, cursing you. You look around. The silver freighter has gone and so have the children. You walk back along the beach and remember the fishermen who played draughts under the palm trees, wagering everything on the game, like politicians who hold the destiny of many in their hands.

COMMENTARY AND NOTES:

Walcott often uses 'I' in his poems, to refer to himself or to the persona in a particular poem. When he uses 'you', as in 'Landfall', it is to refer to another person or to his readers. In this poem, he uses 'you' to refer to himself. This is a colloquial device. We might say, 'You do your best and what do you get?' meaning that we do our best but are not always appreciated. We use 'you' in this way to ally ourselves with others, as much as to say, 'We've all experienced such things.' The only time that he uses 'I' is when he says: 'I am your poet.' In this, he is not the same as other people.

The poem is in three sections: arriving home and being treated as a tourist; realising how he has changed since going away; feeling alone, surrounded by ghosts. The language becomes increasingly simple as he becomes increasingly aware of the realities. His daydreams about going home were as illusory as the stories about ancient Greece.

Afro-Greeks:	the term 'Afro-American' began to be popular in the 1960s. Walcott coins 'Afro-Greeks' to refer to himself and other West Indian children who learned about ancient Greece from their teachers. They knew so much about the Greeks that they were like 'borrowed ancestors'
Helen:	the beautiful Greek wife of Menelaus. She was abducted by the Trojan warrior, Paris, causing the war between the Greeks and the Trojans. After the war, she returned to her homeland, Greece
shades:	spirits, shadows
looms:	Penelope, wife of the Greek, Odysseus, spent her time weaving while her husband was away, vowing that she would not remarry until her tapestry was completed. The weaving stopped when Odysseus returned
doom . . . nights:	nights on the sea as the warriors tried to return to Greece
sea-grape:	(1) bluish edible berry that grows on a plant on sandy shores; (2) sea gooseberry, tiny marine invertebrate, also called 'Venus's girdle'
brittle helmets:	shells
sugar-headed:	with heads like a sugarloaf, i.e. a conical lump of refined sugar, often brown in colour
pot-bellied:	sign of malnutrition
They . . . sore:	they cluster round you, saddening you with their begging
Suffer:	in the New Testament, Christ said, 'Suffer the little children to come unto me, and forbid them not: for of

such is the kingdom of heaven' (Mark 10:14; see also Matthew 19:14 and Luke 18:16)

needle's eye: Christ said, 'It is easier for a camel to go through the eye of a needle, than for a rich man to enter into the kingdom of God' (Matthew 19:24)

you wanted no career: when you were young, you were uninterested in the future

there . . . home: one can go to the place where one was born and still not find the home one was seeking. This is probably because one is really trying to recapture a time, not a place, but although the place may still be there, the time is irrevocably gone

dead . . . draughts: you can almost conjure up the spirits of fishermen who used to play draughts in the shade

eating their islands: playing for large, imaginary sums of money. There is also the suggestion that the greedy may have 'eaten up' the goods that the islands had to offer

---

'Nearing Forty'

SUMMARY:
I have been awake since 4 a.m. listening to the rain and thinking that I am approaching 40, a time of middle age and reduced vision when you should be grateful for an occasional flicker of the poetic flame that once burnt brightly. You who once felt you could chart the meteors will be glad to strike any light, glad to accept your limitations. You'll notice a drop in your creative productivity and become more ordinary. Or perhaps you'll write differently, but still well until you die, aware that inspiration, like any talent, may wither.

COMMENTARY AND NOTES:
Samuel Johnson (1709–84) was a poet, essayist and dictionary maker, who expressed the view that youthful elation and physical pleasure are often replaced by mature reflection and the pleasures of the mind. Many mature poets feel that they can no longer recapture their early insights, enthusiasms and inspiration. Wordsworth wrote about his sense of loss in several poems, including 'Tintern Abbey'. In his youth, his love of nature was an active passion: 'That time is past,/And all its aching joys are now no more,/And all its dizzy raptures.' In maturity, he lost some of his 'vision', and yet added: 'for such loss, I would believe,/Abundant recompense.' Walcott, in this poem, experiences the loss Wordsworth described, but not, as yet, the sense of any compensatory insights.

This 32-line poem is composed of only one sentence, almost as if Walcott needs to rush to set down his feelings. It expresses sadness for the loss of poetic powers and yet it reveals a mastery of form and style that suggests the 'loss' has indeed been compensated for. The metre is regular; the rhyme scheme is a mixture of masculine and feminine rhyme ('rain', 'pane' and 'narrow', 'marrow'); the alliteration ('s' and 'k') echoes the rhythm of the rain and the growing realisation that poetic powers can fade; and the repetition of sounds ('ee' in 'metred', 'weak', 'bleak', 'bleaching') and of words ('rain', 'nearer', 'work') reinforces the point that there is no escape from the passage of time.

Comment was made on the use of pronouns in 'Homecoming: Anse La Raye' and they are also worthy of examination in this poem, where the poet uses 'I' to refer to himself as an individual, 'you' when talking to himself about the past, when he was almost a different person, and 'we' when thinking about himself and his friends at school.

Nearing Forty: the title sets the tone for the poem. It is often thought that writing poetry is a young person's pursuit. To be 40 is to be middle-aged. The vigour and intensity of youth have gone and the philosophical advantages of old age have not yet arrived

weak/vision: Walcott lists some of the penalties of middle age, among them poorer sight. For him, the 'vision' is not just eyesight, but the poetic vision which allows one to see aspects of life in a new way

false dawn: a transient light that appears in the sky before sunrise, sometimes mistaken for dawn. The metaphoric meaning is of achievement that looks less impressive with hindsight

searing meteor: heavenly body that could burn itself into one's mind in the same way that a well-written poem can

dry . . . kettle: a whistling-kettle that is badly dented will not produce a clean, shrill noise. Walcott suggests that he is no longer capable of the unpremeditated productions of the past. There may also be a reference here to a kettle-drum, a percussion instrument whose note changes if the tension of the skin is altered

louvre's gap: louvre windows have narrow, horizontal slats. They can be adjusted so that they can admit different amounts of light and air. The narrower the gap is, the less light is allowed in

watching your leaves thin: seeing how your writing has diminished in size. There is possibly also a suggestion of baldness here

prodigious cynicism: distrust of others. 'Prodigious' suggests a great quantity of cynicism. It also suggests that the cynicism may be threatening to the poet and to others

greenhorns:	US slang for 'innocent', 'young' and perhaps 'gullible'
convectional:	we learn about 'convectional' air currents (i.e. how warm air rises) in geography classes. Walcott suggests that young schoolchildren may use incorrect terms. 'Conventional' (that is, following accepted customs) might be used by children because it is more widespread. There is, of course, the implication that poets can follow either a conventional or a convectional course, the latter leading them into the stratosphere
sadder joy:	this phrase is almost a contradiction in terms. It relates to Wordsworth's view that sadness and experience may reduce our ability to take instinctive pleasure in life and nature. The instinctive pleasure may be replaced by more mature pleasures
as the . . . weep:	Walcott suggests that poets may measure their talent as coolly as a water-clerk may measure the amount of rain that falls. The poet may miss poetic cause and effect in the same way that the water-clerk is unaware that the rain may be caused by the tidal influences of the new moon. The moon, seen through the rain, may appear to weep.

Another Life

This volume of poetry includes many of the themes we have already met in other volumes: alienation, poetic inspiration, love, and the history of the Caribbean. It is essentially autobiographical.

Extract from 'The Divided Child', Chapter 1. I

SUMMARY:
I begin with the sea and will write until all is told or until inspiration fades. I'll begin at twilight when the bugle announces that the flag is to be lowered before sunset and when the golden light casts a spell on the place and the people. That was your heaven and it produced a prodigy, albeit a black prodigy. (As the poet looks back, he sees the past unwinding, like a film. The tense changes from present to past and the pronoun from 'I' to 'he'.) All afternoon, the student had painted the harbour. With the coming of dusk, a girl appeared in a doorway. She and all else seemed still. The painting needed to be finished but the girl was a living work of art, framed by the golden light in the doorway. The picture faded with darkness but the girl could be imagined lighting a fire in the kitchen. As darkness spread,

and as a moon rose in the sky, he went back to the studio. This memory is like a mirror that reflects the past and a time when local people overvalued whiteness and longed for trust between the communities. The moon rose higher, bathing every place with a whiter light as he passed her house. She was like a painting from an earlier age. Inside, a man sat reading. He was brown, going bald and had a jutting jaw and thick glasses. The teacher looked at the sketch and modified it with a few strokes.

COMMENTARY AND NOTES:

This section of the autobiography is organised as a series of word pictures. Each stanza modifies the previous picture, adding detail or moving on. We are introduced to three characters: the poet as a young painter, the beautiful girl who is later named 'Anna', and the teacher who encouraged him to be a painter. The pictures change and develop as the source of light alters, from the amber of sunset, through the silvery whiteness of moonlight, to the paleness of an electric light bulb. The changes are detailed in the repeated and alternating use of words to describe light – 'wane', 'glare', 'drunk with light', 'locked in amber', 'gleam', 'a bulb haloed'.

The sense of freedom that the poet wishes to exercise in calling up the past is reflected in the structure of the poem. It is subtly but not obviously patterned. The rhythm varies from dimeter (two strong stresses): 'The vision died'; to hexameter (six strong stresses): 'a moon ballooned up from the Wireless Station. O'; the rhyme varies from full end rhyme ('died' and 'simplified'); to half-rhyme ('inlet' and 'light'); eye rhyme ('declined' and 'wind'); alliteration links sets of words such as 'glare', 'glaze', 'gleam' or 'book', 'begin', 'bulb'; and assonance uses the 'I' sound to connect 'life', 'I', 'like', 'twilight', 'tired', 'fire' and 'climbed'.

a shut book: normally, when one reveals biographical details, one's life becomes 'an open book'. Walcott revitalises the cliché, suggesting that he will reveal all he knows about the sea until the knowledge is completely shared

moon's filaments: Walcott frequently uses metaphors from modern technology. Here he suggests that the moon's light is like the light given off by the thin tungsten wires that transform electricity into light inside a bulb

glare ... of bugles: dazzling light. When we talk about 'loud' colours, we are applying the description of one sense (hearing) to another (seeing). This is known in poetic terms as 'synaesthesia'. The light is so dazzling as to be 'loud' and thus like the sharp, clear note of bugles

sun ... empire: children in the British Empire used to sing about the Empire on which the sun never set. In other words, the Empire was in all parts of the world

It mesmerized ... wind: there are two references here. (1) In the Old Testament, God spoke to Moses from a bush that burnt but was not consumed by the fire (Exodus 3:2); (2) F. A. Mesmer (1734–1815), who used hypnotism to cure psychological problems, sometimes 'mesmerised' his patients by making them look at the reflection of a light

beer-stein: the towers were round and tall and looked like beer mugs from a distance

locked in amber: insects are sometimes trapped in amber which is a yellowish-brown resin that hardens as it cools

The dream ... monster: a thing that destroys its creator. Frankenstein used his intellect to create a being but it became a monster and destroyed him

sheerly: totally

cinquecento: the sixteenth century in Italian art and literature

amnesia: forgetfulness

moon ballooned: this is a covert reference to the American poet E. E. Cummings (1894–1962) who wrote: 'who cares if the moon's/a balloon'

a generation ... whiteness: many of the people in the West Indies were taught to see white people as superior

chiton-fluted: folded neatly as if in pleats. In ancient Greece and Rome, a 'chiton' was a loose tunic, often in folds from the shoulder. A chiton can also be a small shellfish

alternating ivories: piano keys where white alternates with black

tonsure: the shaved top of a head. Monks often received the tonsure as a mark of their acceptance into the religious life

lacertilian: a reptile. The teacher, Harold Simmons, whom Walcott commemorates, committed suicide. Walcott uses the same phrase, 'a lacertilian jut to his underlip', when describing his teacher in other sections of *Another Life*

Extract from 'Homage to Gregorias', Chapter 8, (part of) I and II

SUMMARY:

I

In that year, Gregorias and his soldier father lived in a ramshackle bungalow, between the town and the forest. Its wooden floors and steps had rotted. Gregorias had screened off half of the verandah for a studio which contained a three-legged table, empty paint-tubes, rum and copies of the works of famous artists. One day, the old soldier fell through the floor of the verandah and was suspended by the waist. Gregorias laughed about it and told the story, but the old man felt ashamed and died within a year. Gregorias was angry and wanted his anger at people's curiosity to be reflected on his father's headstone. We were now both without fathers and were often drunk on whatever alcohol or alcoholic substitute we could find. We thought of ourselves as young artists and modelled our work on Van Gogh, Cézanne and Gauguin. We spent days out in the sun and Gregorias even tried to paint under water. Days merged as we walked and drank and painted.

II

We determined that we would never leave St Lucia until we had captured every part of the island on canvas. We walked and painted from every vantage point and the happiness I felt was almost painful. We were in harmony with the beauty of our surroundings and felt that our success was inevitable.

COMMENTARY AND NOTES:
These sections are a lyrical recreation of an adolescent period, when Walcott and his friend were at one with each other, with the painters they hoped to emulate and with the natural beauty of St Lucia. The dominant image is of a golden, intoxicated haze, part of which may be because an older, wiser, more realistic Walcott is looking back. The style is free, unfettered by overly regular rhyme or rhythm. Yet the ideas run smoothly as if well-rehearsed and the patterning that is missing in the metre is very clear in the vocabulary and imagery. Look, for example, at the section where the old soldier falls through the floor and 'wears' the verandah like a 'belt'. The image of the belt is continued as Gregorias 'buckled' with laughter as he told people the story. And, in the section on the painters, Walcott tries to create in words the imagery that the post-impressionists captured in paint.

Gregorias:	Walcott's school friend, the painter Dunstan St Omer, whom he also calls 'Apilo'
finished soldier:	Gregorias's father. The phrase has at least two meanings: (1) a complete, excellent soldier; (2) a soldier without any hope of further success
treaders:	steps
exhausted:	(1) used up; (2) tubes of paint that the artist used, exhausting himself in the process
a lowering quart:	a steadily reducing amount of rum. A quart is two pints or just over one litre
rum:	rum is brewed in the West Indies. It is also a traditional drink of sailors

drunk:	the repetition of 'drunk' recalls Milton's description of the Philistines in *Samson Agonistes* (1671): 'When their hearts were jocund and sublime/Drunk with idolatry, drunk with wine'
turpentine:	this is a spirit used for cleaning brushes and painted surfaces but it was also drunk by the poor because of its very high alcohol content
absinthe:	strong, green alcohol, often mixed with water
tannic Canaries muscatel:	a strong wine containing tannic acid, a preservative
Van Gogh:	Vincent Van Gogh (1853–90), a Dutch post-impressionist painter, best known for such paintings as 'Sunflowers', 'Cornfield with Crows' and 'Cornfield and Cypresses'
Cézanne:	Paul Cézanne (1839–1906), a French post-impressionist painter who was a major influence on modern art, especially cubism
Aix:	Aix-en-Provence in southern France, where Cézanne was born and did much of his work
Gauguin:	Paul Gauguin (1848–1903), a French post-impressionist painter who lived and painted in the West Indies and the South Pacific
yams:	large tubers, also known as sweet potatoes
whole-suit:	(1) fully dressed; (2) wholeheartedly, without reservation
Trades:	the winds that blow between the Tropics and the Equator
combers:	long, curling waves
while . . . mirages:	while the heat made the tar on the roads melt, causing it to reflect the colours of the rainbow
astigmatic saint:	short-sighted saint, saint with poor vision
goyave . . . sapotille:	types of trees
pennons:	flags tapered at one end
sanderlings:	small sandpipers

Extract from 'A Simple Flame', Chapter 15. I–III

SUMMARY:

I

I still think about you and still miss you. I see you in the faces of schoolgirls and you smile your forgiveness. You always seemed to be surrounded by protective sisters. It is 20 years since you were my first love and even though we are now middle-aged, you appear in photographs I have taken, sometimes clear, sometimes indistinct, laughing but lifeless.

Thinking about you, I think about literature. You were a living novel, a composite of all the Annas I've read about, all the Annas who, in spite of love, had to say 'goodbye'. Even then, you were a doomed heroine and you knew it.

II

Who were you? Pasternak's heroine as you performed your tasks about the house? Twenty years on, something I read reminds me of you. I have written about you, perhaps killing something between us. Even the closest may have to part but something is left behind like an awareness of silence after a thunderstorm.

III

I knew you would tire of St Lucia and you did, going to England to train as a nurse. I used to imagine you like a nurse in war films walking to your hospital. You never got married. A woman should not read love poems written 20 years too late, but I have written this to honour you. When my vows and affections were diminishing, you moved on.

COMMENTARY AND NOTES:
Anna is the young poet's first love and she, too, receives extensive treatment in *Another Life*. As you read the sections devoted to Anna, you might wish to think about whether she is ever realised as completely as an individual as Gregorias is. Perhaps she was more of a symbol than a person with whom he has been intimate? Perhaps he is in love with the thought of a boy being in love for the first time? And yet, this is a moving evocation of young love that is doomed and a tribute to a girl who found it necessary to seek 'another heaven'. The poem is written in short, free-verse stanzas. It gives the impression of a spontaneous lyrical outpouring, but a close reading reveals it to be highly patterned. The rhythm changes from quietly reflective to emotionally charged. There are still many unanswered questions, many words and thoughts that recur. The words and images associated with Anna fall into five main categories which overlap: home ('house', 'kitchen', 'laundry', 'chickens', 'cabbage garden', 'rabbits', 'clotheslines', 'folded linen'); nature ('rainy', 'thorn thicket', 'autumn', 'fire', 'wheatfields', 'marsh edge', 'shallows', 'flamingoes', 'birches', 'snowdrift', 'gulls', 'herons', 'wind', 'stones', 'grass'); Russian literature ('Russia', 'Karenina', 'Revolution', 'commissar', 'Akhmatova', 'Pasternaks'); religion ('sisters', 'signs', 'iconography', 'novitiate', 'church', 'nuns', 'communion', 'communicant', 'candle', 'vows', 'heaven'); human love ('smile', 'ripening pears', 'mellowing breasts', 'darkened house', 'virginal', 'first love', 'bride', 'married', 'aisle', 'register', 'vows'). In spite of all the information provided, however, Anna remains passive, frozen like the Anna in the photographs.

your ... faces: your face is no longer clearly distinguishable but merges with those of all schoolgirls

forgiveness: Walcott feels that he needs to be forgiven by Anna, possibly because he did not treat her as well as he should have

sisters: (1) siblings; (2) nuns. Most schools in St Lucia were run by Catholics

rain season: sunshine is one of the key images in the evocation of the friendship in 'Homage to Gregorias'. In this section, it is rain. The rainy season in St Lucia normally occurs half-way through the year

war: Walcott knew Anna during and just after the Second World War. This other war is probably the Vietnam War which ended when US troops were withdrawn in 1973

our imitation autumn: the third segment of our lives, that is, middle age

In that hair ... another country: notice that Anna is often described by images which compare her with inanimate objects: fruit, another country, rain. She is equated with nature and, consequently, dehumanised and depersonalised. She also becomes all the other Annas of fiction, loved perhaps more for what she represented than for what she was

unbearably clear-eyed: were the eyes too hard to look into because of their beauty or because the young poet could not fully meet her gaze?

Christie, Karenina: Julie Christie played the heroine in the film version (1965) of Boris Pasternak's *Doctor Zhivago* (1958); *Anna Karenina* (1875–6) is the title of a novel by Leo Tolstoy

The golden commissar: another reference to *Doctor Zhivago*, a novel dealing with the Russian Revolution of 1917. A 'commissar' was an official of the Communist Party, responsible for education

Akhmatova: Anna Akhmatova (1889–1966) was a Russian poet, renowned for her love lyrics

thrumming: rhythmic noise like the strumming of a guitar

sunder: move apart, break away

iconography: the symbols used in a work of art; a collection of pictures, often of Christ

riffling: flicking or sifting through to pick out precious items

novitiate: probationary period before a young woman becomes a nun. While they are novices, the women wear white veils

communicant:	one who is at peace with the Church and is thus allowed to receive Holy Communion
your ... linen:	your beliefs carefully tended. Linens used for Holy Communion have to be washed, ironed and folded in a particular way
candle-like:	bringing light into darkness; also possibly 'alone'. The suggestion of 'aloneness' is reinforced by the reference to 'virginal' and to carrying 'oneself' down the aisle. Normally, a couple goes down the aisle and the bridegroom carries the bride over the threshold

Extract from 'The Estranging Sea', Chapter 23. IV

SUMMARY:

I named you Gregorias because its sound summoned up thoughts of the pounding surf and of painted frescoes. You were like a black Greek, like a sun that marvelled at its own heat and light. Our time spent together is remembered with intensity. We were special, secure, godlike. We were like newly created Adams with the task of creating our world in our image. You were like Renaissance man, painting brown rather than white cherubs and capturing St Lucia on your canvas.

COMMENTARY AND NOTES:

Walcott ends *Another Life* as he began it, contemplating the sea and painting. It is significant that the very last person mentioned is not Anna but Gregorias. In this section, there is a structured outpouring of emotion; full rhyme returns with 'Masaccio', 'window', 'flow' and 'Apilo'; half-rhyme appears in 'because' and 'frescoes'; consonance in 'old' and 'invented'; sound patterns are specifically referred to by Walcott with regard to the name 'Gregorias' and these are picked up in 'Greek' and 'glow', 'blest', 'black' and 'blaze', 'shamed' and 'shadow'. Perhaps the most obvious pattern, however, is the repetition, often at the end of lines, of words and images associated with light and fire ('explosive', 'sun', 'blaze', 'fire', 'lit', 'light', 'star', 'glow').

we ... world:	this is almost intentionally blasphemous in that Christ is referred to as 'Lux Mundi', the light of the world
Adam's task:	in the Book of Genesis, Adam was placed in charge of the natural world and given the task of naming animals, birds and fish (Genesis 2:19)
Renaissance:	period that bridges the Middle Ages and the modern world. The Renaissance was a period of the rebirth of culture and learning, usually said to have started in Italy at the beginning of the fourteenth century

Giotto:	an Italian painter (?1266–1337). His works include frescoes in Assisi, Florence and Padua
Masaccio:	an Italian painter (1401–?28). His frescoes are in Florence
wooden star:	painter's easel

Sea Grapes

'Adam's Song'

SUMMARY:

In our day, adulteresses are killed by gossip, not stoning. The first woman was Eve. She was tempted by the devil in the form of the serpent. Her sin makes the entire human race guilty, or else Eve is innocent. Since the beginning of time, nothing has changed. Men still sing of their love of women, just as Adam did, even though he knew their sin would result in their death. Adam's song, in part, makes amends to God. In it he tells Eve that she is part of him and he loves her.

COMMENTARY AND NOTES:

This beautifully organised lyric needs little explanation. The two four-lined stanzas, with which it opens and closes, are complete sentences, rhymed *a b a b*, and, although they are rhythmically different, they are both symmetrical. A knowledge of the Book of Genesis would form a useful backdrop to this love poem, but even without such knowledge of the Bible, the religious vocabulary of love, sin and repentance is evident.

The ... death:	in the New Testament, Christ saved the life of an adulteress who, according to Mosaic Law, could have been stoned to death. He told the men who planned to stone her: 'He that is without sin among you, let him first cast a stone at her' (John 8:7)
that ... slime:	that ruin her character and accuse her of all kinds of perversion
horned:	betrayed sexually. In the Old Testament, the 'horn' was a symbol of power ('In my name shall his horn be exalted' (Psalm 89:24)); Moses is sometimes described as having 'horns of light'; and the devil, too, is depicted as having horns
everyone guilty:	according to traditional Christian belief, all children are born into the world in a state of Original Sin because of the sin of Eve. She was tricked by the Serpent into eating fruit from the Tree of Knowledge of Good and Evil

against:	(1) in opposition to; (2) in defiance of; (3) as a protection from
lights:	panthers' eyes, like cats' eyes, reflect light at night
his . . . trees:	Adam's death, like that of Eve, was the punishment for disobeying God. He had forbidden them to eat the fruit from one tree in the Garden of Eden. Once they had eaten this fruit they were condemned to leave the Garden, to earn 'their bread' by the 'sweat of their brow', and to die
jealousy:	in the Old Testament, God is described as 'a jealous God' (Exodus 20:5). Adam, by eating the fruit, had put his love for Eve above his love for God
who wipes his eyes:	there are two suggestions here: (1) God cried when Adam and Eve betrayed him but found solace and consolation in Adam's song. (Walcott may be covertly commending the role of the poet.) (2) God wipes Adam's eyes because his anger has been assuaged by the song
Heart:	Adam's term of address for Eve who was, according to Genesis 2:21–2, made from one of his ribs

---

'Parades, Parades'

SUMMARY:

We have control of the land, sea and air now and yet people and politicians follow the well-known lines, established by others in the past. There is little difference between colonial government and independence, in spite of all the independence parades. Why is there bewilderment and fear in the eyes of the innocent? Were we better off under colonial rule? We are still waiting for fundamental change. Here he comes, Papa Doc Duvalier of Haiti, followed by his well-fed, expensively dressed cabinet. Who can call the silence that he inspires respect? How did this state of affairs come about? Why did I acquiesce in it?

COMMENTARY AND NOTES:

This poem is in complete contrast to 'Adam's Song'. It leaves the realms of love and religion for the world of selfish and destructive politics. It is thematically similar to 'The Great Day' (1938) by W. B. Yeats:

Hurrah for revolution and more cannon-shot!
A beggar upon horseback lashes a beggar on foot.
Hurrah for revolution and cannon come again!
The beggars have changed places, but the lash goes on.

Both these poems use irony; they both suggest that there is little to choose between one government and the government that replaces it; and they both use repetition. Walcott's repetition is indicated in the title, in the repetition of 'parades' in the poem, and in the exploitation of vocabulary to suggest the movement and noise of parades ('marches', 'circling', 'brazen joy', 'tubas', 'drummed', 'dais').

There is a growing sense of desperation in this poem. The first stanza suggests that a change of government has not meant a change of heart. Stanza 2 suggests that the colonial government might even have been preferable. Stanza 3 looks at the example of Haiti, at the adulation demanded by its dictator, and asks how such a situation could have come about and how the intellectuals could have allowed it to happen.

pads of old caravans: no one walks in the desert unless they follow the tracks established by the nomads, who have traversed the deserts for centuries

keels . . . parallels: the boats appear to cut tracks in the oceans. They too follow navigation 'lines' that are indicated on maps

the blue . . . mountains: planes can now fly in the sky above the mountains. They also follow flight paths

politicians . . . garden: politicians continue in the same arid way as before, not taking advantage of the new opportunities opening before them

gri-gri: African talisman; tree from which carved amulets are made. There is a possible pun here in that 'gri' is a form of 'agree' and so, by implication, the politicians are 'yes-men'

desiccating: drying out, dehydrating

like goats: goats can be very destructive to the environment. They eat not only leaves but roots as well. Some environmentalists blame the desertification of North Africa on the large herds of goats kept there

White Papers: official government reports

Whitehall: London site of the main British Government offices

plumed white cork-hat: ceremonial hat of the Governor-General of the island

when . . . away: when the seat of government was in London and not in the Caribbean

veiled queen: Queen Victoria, often depicted wearing a veil, symbolising her widowhood

Papa: François 'Papa Doc' Duvalier (1907–71), the dictator of Haiti, who ran the country with brutal ruthlessness. His ministers often wore black dinner suits

as the . . . mountain: as the wind, the symbol of inspiration and energetic reappraisal, is like a dog that puts its tail between its legs in fear

forced, hoarse hosannas: the shouts of acclamation for the new leaders have been well practised but are not sincerely felt

'Names'

SUMMARY:

My race began countless years ago before language existed. Now my race is here in the Caribbean. I began with no past and no future and I have much in common with people, especially oppressed people, from other parts of the world. My race began with a cry, with a primeval word. My history is lost, wiped out like words written in the sand and eradicated by the sea. When people gave names to these bays, was it because they were lonely for the countries they had left or in mockery of the untamed land? They left beautiful places to come here and the loss made them bitter. They felt they had the right to give the names of the Old World to places in the New World. The Africans accepted their fate, learned the language of the colonisers, and changed it. The natural world here is greater than the man-made glories in Europe. The only enemy is death, which has always reigned supreme throughout the world. Children, look at the stars over the Caribbean, not at the ones that can be seen over Europe. What do they look like? Sir, they look like fireflies trapped in black syrup.

COMMENTARY AND NOTES:

There is an old tradition that knowing a name gives us power over the person or thing named. This is a partial explanation of God's answer to Moses in the Old Testament. God described himself as 'I am who am'. To have given a name would have been to lose some of his power and mystery. In this poem, Walcott suggests that there is a link between the language one uses and one's sense of identity. Perhaps European languages suggested divisions between people that other languages did not stress. And even when Africans learned European languages, they modified them so that they reflected an African heritage. This is clear when the child is asked to say what he sees in the sky. African and European see the same thing but they describe it in different ways.

This 83-line poem is in two sections, the first dealing with unrecorded history, the second with the colonisation of the New World. Walcott is interested in the ways that language can empower speakers. The first human utterances were vowels, like birds' cries, like 'I', and yet the very choice of vowel was an expression of identity. Later came the nouns, the 'sea', the 'horizon', the 'tongue', the 'stars'. Without language, there can be no memory. The first part uses repetition a great deal, as a means of suggesting the development of language. There is repetition of sounds ('s' and 'z' and 'b' and 'm'), repetition of words ('race', 'began', 'no'), and repetition of phrases ('the goldsmith from Benares' etc.). The second part uses contrast, the man-made structures of Europe and the natural beauties of the West Indies, European words imposed on West Indian places and fruit. Throughout the poem, there is a developing equation between language ('nouns', 'vowel', 'inflections') and identity ('my race', 'my children') and the final statement is given to a child, who may be poor and forced to use a language that is not his own, but who sees with the eyes of a poet, and has the courage to say what he sees.

My race began:	according to modern scholarship, our species began in East Africa several million years ago
no nouns:	in the Book of Genesis, Adam is given the task of naming the world and all in it (Genesis 2:19–20). Without names, there are no nouns. The word 'noun' comes from 'nom', meaning 'name'
with . . . stars:	in Africa, the stars seem to be in a different position
Levantine:	'the Levant' used to describe an area of the Middle East. It was composed of parts of modern Israel, Lebanon and Syria. Levantine traders were well known in commercial circles
when . . . horizon:	before Columbus's journey in 1492, the western horizon was seen as the end of the world for most Europeans, although half the world lay beyond the horizon. Walcott goes on to show that the division was a mirage and that people beyond that 'division' lived and worked, unaware that they were unknown
Benares:	a city in India, renowned for its fine work in gold and precious metals
Canton:	a port in China
mirror . . . behind:	many people believed that their souls could be trapped by a mirror, if they looked into it too much. Similarly, many believed that cameras could trap the souls of the people whose photographs had been taken
Benin:	the centre of a flourishing culture in West Africa before the Europeans explored the area. It is famous for its bronze sculptures
sea-eagle:	fish-eating eagle
osprey:	large, fish-eating bird of prey, often called a fish-hawk
foreclosed:	(1) shut out, barred; (2) claimed exclusive rights to
courts of Castile:	the royal court of Ferdinand and Isabella was in the northern Spanish city of Castile. It was from this court in 1492 that Christopher Columbus set off to find a new route to the Indies. Instead, he found the 'West Indies'

Versailles:	Louis XIV built a palace at Versailles, near Paris, which was the envy of other European monarchs
Corinthian crests:	Corinth was a city state in ancient Greece. Corinthian crests are carvings at the tops of pillars. The carvings are representations of acanthus leaves
Valencia:	(1) city port in Spain, the capital of the Moorish kingdom; the region is famous for oranges; (2) city in Venezuela
Mayaro:	a beach in Trinidad
baie-la:	'the bay' in St Lucian creole French
worm . . . helmet:	the worm is not a warrior, but it survives when warriors die
Orion:	the constellation which is also known as 'The Hunter'. It contains two very bright stars, Betelgeuse and Rigel
Arabs:	the derogatory term 'street Arabs' is used for children, often orphans, who make a living by begging on the streets
molasses:	black syrup

The Star-Apple Kingdom

'The Schooner *Flight*', Chapters 5 and 11

Chapter 5: 'Shabine Encounters the Middle Passage'
I'm busy making coffee in the ship's kitchen first thing in the morning, when the fog thickens into the sails of many sailing ships. Our schooner was floating in the middle of a whole fleet of ships where the crews were dead men. On the decks I saw famous admirals and I heard their commands. The ships passed through us and faded as the mist disappeared. Then we passed slave ships, bearing the flags of all countries. Our ancestors were down below deck but they could not hear our shouts. Tomorrow, we will be in Barbados.

COMMENTARY AND NOTES:
This extract is taken from a long narrative poem, made up of 11 sections. It tells the story of Shabine, a sailor who travels between the islands on a schooner. He left his home in Trinidad for many reasons: he needed to earn money; he was offended by the growth of materialism; he was cheated by a politician; and he wanted to escape from the rows with his mistress Maria Concepcion. Like many journeys, Shabine's can be taken literally; or it may be seen as a metaphor for our journey through life; or it may even represent the poet's dedication to his art, in spite of the pain it brings.

On a foggy morning, he has a vision of a fleet of ships, associated with great naval battles of the past and including ships containing African slaves. A useful exercise might be to read Samuel Taylor Coleridge's 'The Rime of the Ancient Mariner' (1798) and to compare Shabine's experience with the Ancient Mariner's. The first eight lines of this extract are written in creole English. We notice 'I brisk' rather than 'I was brisk' (1.1), 'l'il' for 'little' (1.2) and ' 'cause' for 'because' (1.4), and the unmarked form of the verbs 'coil', 'swirl', 'swell' and 'grip'. In this way, Walcott creates the impression of an ordinary man presenting us with an extraordinary vision. As Shabine describes what he saw, he uses images from nature ('forest', 'leaves', 'sunlight', 'waves', 'grass', 'weeds'), from seafaring ('cannons', 'crews', 'frigates', 'barkentines', 'current', 'admirals', 'masts', 'stern', 'below deck') and compares the ships sailing on the surface of the earth to buckets on a water wheel.

There is little overt rhyme in this extract, although we find it in 'sea' and 'see', 'suppose' and 'knows'. There is, however, a considerable amount of half-rhyme ('dawn' and 'down', 'skull' and 'beautiful', 'cannons' and 'bones') and a great deal of sound play as in the use of hard 'g' and 'k' in the first eight lines. The vision is given extra credibility by the use of Shabine's natural speech and by the unemotional ending: 'Tomorrow our landfall will be the Barbados.' There is no authorial comment on the savagery of warfare and the slave trade. Readers are left to draw their own conclusions.

the Middle Passage: the journey of the slaves from Africa to the New
                World. See also 'Laventille'
Man: general term of friendly address, not necessarily to a
                man
it was horrors ... beautiful: the vision frightened Shabine but he was
                aware of its beauty. This use of oxymoron (bringing
                together terms which almost contradict each other) is
                frequently used for emphasis. W. B. Yeats uses a
                similar technique in 'Easter, 1916' (1923) when he
                says: 'A terrible beauty is born'
behind the glass: the ships were like those constructed inside a bottle
frigates: square-rigged warships
barkentines: large sailing ships with three masts
Rodney: George Brydges Rodney (1719–92), English admiral
Nelson: Horatio Nelson (1758–1805), English admiral
de Grasse: François Joseph Paul de Grasse (1722–88), French
                admiral
Shabines: all the people, especially sailors, with whom Shabine
                identifies
weeds: (1) seaweed; (2) clothes worn as a sign of mourning

water wheel: (1) a wheel with buckets attached for raising water from a stream; (2) a simple turbine which uses water to drive machinery

Who knows ... name?: in a world where people have been taken away from their homes and enslaved, people cannot be sure who their grandparents were or what they were called

Chapter 11: 'After the Storm'

There is a strange light that follows a storm and, in that light, I saw Maria Concepcion marrying the sea. Since then, I have wanted nothing. There was a light shower of rain falling on my face, and the sea was calm. Fall gently, rain, on the sea and make the islands as pure as they once were. Let everything smell clean and fresh. I have stopped dreaming. Whatever happens, nature will provide for my needs. Although my ship will never venture beyond the Caribbean Sea, I shall be content if I have given voice to the sadness of others. Open the map. There are many islands, of different sizes, in the Caribbean. There are over 1000 in the Bahamas alone. From the front of the schooner, I bless them all. I yearn to find the perfect island, where suffering does not exist, but there are so many islands here, as many as there are stars in the sky! Life goes on as it always has done. My first love was the sea. Now, it is my last love. I work and read and try to forget that happiness ever existed. Sometimes, at night, there is only me and the sea and the sky.

COMMENTARY AND NOTES:

This section of 'The Schooner *Flight*' is written in an approximation to West Indian creole that is simple, subtle and lyrical. Using it, Shabine manages to create in words the human need to find a peace of mind that transcends the need for personal fulfilment: 'I try to forget what happiness was,/and when that don't work, I study the stars.'

Maria Concepcion: Shabine's mistress. The name is derived from 'Mary, the Immaculate Conception', a reference to the belief that the mother of Jesus was not born with Original Sin. She alone, of all human beings, was 'immaculate', that is, without stain

she just ... drizzle: when people used a flat iron for pressing clothes, they often sprinkled water on the garment

I finish dream: I have finished with dreaming

inland sea: the Caribbean Sea, 'surrounded' by South America, Central America, Mexico, the United States and the chain of West Indian islands

one thousand: a slight exaggeration, unless we count rocks as islands

Bahamas: a group of over 700 coral islands

keys:	(1) quays, wharves; (2) islands, such as the Florida Keys; (3) entry into the Caribbean
bowsprit:	a spar projecting from the front of a sailing boat

'Sabbaths, W.I.'

SUMMARY:
Sad, sleepy villages – faded volcanoes – dried banana leaves, polluted river, cocoa grove in which even the birds forget to sing – trees peeling in the heat – a dead lizard – rivers that move slowly and quietly – dry esplanade where old men play draughts and ships pass by – hills that look useless, dry ferns, roads that seem to lead nowhere – crabs that are almost motionless – herons checking their appearance in the water – nettles – Sundays when even a light at the end of the road was a talking point – Sundays when mother rested and the sisters prayed and everything passed us by.

COMMENTARY AND NOTES:
This 31-line poem has only one capital letter and no full stops. It has no sentences, just thoughts strung together like a litany that rehearses the boredom of village life on a Sunday long ago. It is composed of images, most of them static (the dog is sleeping; the lizard is dead) or no longer useful ('burnt', 'broken', 'forgotten', 'peeling', 'spittle', 'stuck'). The fact that there are no finished sentences reflects the boredom of a time and place where nothing seemed to happen. The fact that words and phrases are repeated stresses the monotonous recurrence of the Sundays in St Lucia when Walcott was young.

melancholia:	mental state characterised by depression and irrational fears and worries
ochre:	a yellowish-red colour, produced from pigments in the clay
volcanoes:	St Lucia is a volcanic island
ashen roses:	(1) roses drained of colour; (2) roses which are covered in volcanic ash; (3) 'Ashes of Roses' was a cheap but popular perfume
incurable ... poverty:	this may be a reference to Christ's claim: 'The poor ye have with ye always' (John 12:18); or to the adage: 'There are two things that cannot be hidden: poverty and wealth'
yellow sulphur stone:	stone thrown out by the volcanoes
broken bottles:	much of the rubbish was dumped in the river
whose cry ... yellow:	many poets, including Charles Baudelaire (1821–67), an important influence on Walcott, experimented with a device known as 'synaesthesia', by which the

characteristics of one sensory domain are carried over to another. For example, the adjective 'loud' logically applies to what we hear, but when we talk about a 'loud colour' we are applying it to what we see

gommiers:	gum trees
the dead . . . stone:	lizards frequently change their colour to blend in with their surroundings. They are often a blue-grey colour when dead
spittle:	saliva
esplanade:	long, level stretch of ground beside a beach
frigate birds:	tropical birds like cormorants, also called 'man-o'-war birds'
vespers:	evening, the time for evening prayers in a religious house

---

'The Saddhu of Couva'

SUMMARY:

At sunset, a brass gong sounds in Couva and I sit quietly, meditating. My soul stays close by in the course of my meditation because India is too far away for it to make the journey. The sun-tinged clouds are my monks; the drone of mosquitoes is the musical accompaniment to my prayers. I don't put on a white turban to pray but my hands are old like the pages of the holy book. I can remember India but I do not miss it because I brought it with me. But time passes and customs change. Young people are more interested in the cinema than in their prayers. When I was on the Council I talked to no avail. Old people are no longer revered for their wisdom. My friends blame the government but I think it may be a more serious problem. Maybe the gods are too old to be effective. Maybe they are dead or have been captured. Maybe modern technology has killed our need for gods. It is sunset. My mind is teeming with thoughts. I go upstairs, where my sandalwood bed is a link with the past.

COMMENTARY AND NOTES:

This is one of the many poems in which Walcott deals with a serious subject humorously. The holy man of Couva sees society from his point of view, but shrewdly addresses problems faced by society worldwide.

The form of language used for the Saddhu's monologue is Trinidad creole English. It is easy to understand and sensitively recreates the particular language of an old man at odds with modern life.

The four stanzas are written in free verse, where the lines and the stanzas are of unequal length and reflect thoughts that refuse to be pigeon-holed. There is no rhyme, but considerable repetition of sounds and words.

The . . . Couva: the holy man of Couva, a village in Trinidad

is then . . . soul:	that is when I can look into my soul
white cattle bird:	an egret, a type of heron
evening canes:	sugar cane at evening
India:	almost half of the population of Trinidad is of Indian origin
bald . . . robes:	clouds touched with sunset resemble the robes of holy men
Ramlochan:	Indian name of one dedicated to Rama, a reincarnation of Vishnu
mantras:	prayers that are chanted as an aid to meditation
Anopheles:	scientific name for a type of malaria-carrying mosquito
sitar:	a stringed Indian instrument that takes a long time to tune and is plucked like a harp
Divali:	Hindu festival of light to honour the goddess of prosperity
Ramayana:	Hindu holy book which tells the story of Rama and his wife, Sita, in Sanskrit verse
sacred monkeys:	monkeys were sacred to the god Hanuman
Bengal:	region in the north-east of India
Uttar Pradesh:	state in northern India through which the River Ganges runs
as fierce . . . time:	at harvest time, fires are often started in the cane fields to burn the weeds
I will pass . . . unsheathed:	followers of Hinduism believe in reincarnation. One may come back in several forms until one leads such a perfect life that the soul does not need to be reincarnated again
There are . . . elders:	old people are no longer given the respect they deserve
snake-armed god:	possibly Naga-Sanniya, who is sometimes depicted with snake-like arms
Hanuman:	the monkey god in Hindu tradition
like . . . cremation:	'Suttee' was practised in traditional Hindu society. Widows climbed on the funeral pyres of their husbands and were burnt to death

Part 4

Hints for study

Approaching and analysing poetry

Poetry is a form of communication, but, unlike the prose in telephone books, it does not aim to transmit information easily, directly or un-equivocally. It is devised so that it informs the emotions as well as the brain, and it does so by working on several levels. A poem may be interpreted literally, or it may carry metaphorical or even symbolic meanings. In addition, the structures used may be deliberately ambiguous, that is, they may be interpreted in different ways. These points can be illustrated by means of two simple examples.

Looking first of all at words, we can say that in a Christian context the word *shepherd* can refer literally to one who looks after sheep. It may also be used metaphorically of a priest, who looks after a human flock. At a symbolic level, it may imply Christ, the 'pastor' who guards the entire Church.

A good example of structural ambiguity is provided by Yeats in 'He wishes for the cloth of gold'. The poetic persona says, 'I made my song a coat', which can mean both 'I made a coat for my song' and 'I made my song into a coat'. In other words, he may be saying 'I decorated my verse' or 'I protected myself by writing poetry' or, more probably, he is suggesting that both interpretations are valid.

Poetry uses language, but it stretches the language so that it can express 'Thoughts that do often lie too deep for tears' (Wordsworth, 'Intimations of Immortality').

When we read poetry, therefore, we should be aware that the poet uses all the resources of the language, its sounds, its words, its structures and its meanings, to create a many-layered entity. Only close acquaintance with a poem will begin to reveal all that the poet has included.

Some people worry that they will destroy the magic of a poem if they analyse it too closely. They regard a poem as being fragile, like a butterfly, and ask how taking it apart can possibly help in its appreciation. If a poem were a butterfly, this objection would be valid. Indeed, the analysis would be even more destructive than we have suggested, because we would not be able to put the poem together again. Poetry, however, is not like a delicate living organism that perishes if we look too closely. A better analogy is to compare poetry to people. The longer we know them, and the more we think about them, the better we understand them. Similarly, just as people we thought we knew are capable of surprising us, so great poems never allow us to understand them totally. They continue to have depths that we can only guess at, aspects that we come to appreciate at different times of our life.

A poem is not a puzzle that we attempt to solve, so there is no simple, uniform technique that we can use to break its code. Each poem is unique and must be approached with an open mind and with a willingness to understand the poet's point of view. Although there are no simple rules that will work on each occasion, there are three general comments that should help. First, understanding is based on three stages:

- reading and responding
- checking your response
- evaluating

Often, when we read a poem, we are not absolutely clear what it means. We can recognise strong emotion, perhaps fear or anger, depression or exhilaration, love or frustration. This is what we mean by 'responding'. We can respond to poetry at an emotional level, before we respond intellectually. It is similar, in a way, to our reaction to music, which can make us feel cheerful, relaxed or sad.

When we have noted our response, we should check it to see if we can support or refine it. If we have sensed fear in the poem, for example, is it because there is a sense of haste? Are there run-on lines which carry us on until we are almost breathless? Are the words associated with fear or dread or suspense or suspicion? Are the sentences disjointed, reflecting disjointed thoughts? Are there any images that can help explain your reaction? Images of darkness, isolation, pain or of weapons? Perhaps, on closer examination, the fear may be replaced by anger. Gradually, by re-reading, we deepen our understanding.

By this stage, we have begun to evaluate the poem, assessing how effectively the poet controls words and images and, through them, our response. The evaluation should not be either mechanical or superficial. It should always be based on our own reactions, reactions which have been informed by a close reading of the text.

Secondly, don't be afraid of terms such as *alliteration, assonance, metaphor, metre, rhyme*, but don't use them loosely. These are technical terms which can help us to comment accurately on aspects of poetic language. Poetry is now *read* more often than it is *heard* but the sound of a poem is like music, and, like music, it can work on our emotions. Knowing the meaning of words like 'alliteration' will not deepen your appreciation of poetry, but it will help you to talk and write about why one particular organisation of words can affect us so much more strongly than another. You should look up these terms in a good dictionary, but, in the next section, short, simple definitions will be provided that will be of help.

Thirdly, remember that you are offering an interpretation of a poem, and that an interpretation is always partial, never complete. That explains why two people can respond strongly, yet differently, to the same poem. As long as you can support your point of view by reference to the text, your evaluation will be valid.

Writing about poetry

Each of us, with practice, evolves our own style. In writing about poetry, however, it may be useful to employ a number of strategies. These are meant as a support for your ideas, not as a substitute for them. Having responded to the poem, checked and evaluated your response, you may feel that it is helpful to write about some or all of the levels of a poem, and we might consider the levels of sound, words, structures and imagery.

First, let us take the level of sound. Remember that we are talking about *sounds* and not *letters*. The same letter can be used to represent different sounds, as is clear if we pronounce the 'c' in 'cat', 'cello' and 'ceiling'. In addition, different letters can be used for the same sound, as in such words as 'come', 'key' and 'quay'. The sound of a poem will always be significant. That is why we have stressed the importance of reading poetry aloud. The four most significant patterns of sound are alliteration, assonance, rhyme and rhythm.

Alliteration involves the repetition of the same consonant sounds:

Full **f**athom **f**ive thy **f**ather lies.'   (Shakespeare, *The Tempest*)

Assonance draws attention to vowels by repeating vowel sounds. We can hear it in the 'I' sound of the words 'five', 'thy' and 'lies' above. *Rhyme* also involves repetition, this time the repetition of a syllable:

And thou in this shalt find thy monu**ment**,
When tyrants' crests and tombs of brass are **spent**.
(Shakespeare, Sonnet CVII)

All natural speech is rhythmic, but poetry uses *metre*, which is regulated rhythm. If we paraphrased the above couplet from Shakespeare, we might say:

You will be remembered because of my writing when material monuments have disappeared.

The meaning may be similar but the rhythmic couplet is easier to remember. Even if we forget some of the words, we can remember the 'tune'. This 'tune' is the poem's metre.

People impose pattern upon their language so that it will be easier to remember. We all do it. Geography teachers may teach that in Britain we tend to get 'warm, wet, westerly winds in winter'. Advertisers know that

buyers will remember brandnames like **Handy Andies, Fruit 'n' Fibre** and
Tiny Tots. Politicians exploit the mnemonic possibilities of language when
they make pronouncements:

> We shall pay any price, bear any burden, meet any hardship, sup-
> port any friend, oppose any foe, to assure the survival and success of
> liberty.   (John F. Kennedy, 1961)

And poets use all the resources of the language to weld form and meaning
into an inseparable entity.

We often find it easier to deal with words than with sounds, but it is
worth bearing in mind a number of points when discussing the vocabulary
of a poem. First, it is worth remembering that most words carry associations with them. 'Freedom fighter' does not conjure up the same image as
'terrorist' and when we think about it, we become aware of the different
connotations of:

> The Chancellor stated . . .
> The Chancellor insisted . . .
> The Chancellor implied . . .

Poets consciously choose words with specific connotations which they
either reinforce or challenge.

Secondly, we might ask ourselves if the vocabulary is simple or complex; mainly monosyllabic and well known, such as:

> Day after day, day after day,
> We stuck, nor breath nor motion;
> As idle as a painted ship
> Upon a painted ocean.
> (Coleridge, 'The Rime of the Ancient Mariner')

or polysyllabic and less transparent, such as:

> Season of mists and mellow fruitfulness,
> Close bosom-friend of the maturing sun . . .
> (Keats, 'To Autumn')

All poets will, of course, use both, but their choice will always be significant.

Thirdly, it may be of value to consider whether or not the vocabulary
belongs to a particular register, such as love, science, war or technology.
The subject matter influences the choice of words, and in a poem about the
'middle passage', we might expect such words as 'Africa', 'manacle',
'sea', 'separation', 'slave', as well as a sub-register of words relating to
pain.

In examining the structures used by poets, we might ask if they use short
or long sentences, statements, questions, exclamations or negatives. Such

structures covertly influence our responses. We might also look at whether the word order is as we might expect:

I saw three ships.

or modified:

Three ships I saw.

A poem's imagery can influence us, even before we fully understand it. When we think that a poem is gentle or violent, angry or composed, we are often responding to the poet's use of imagery. Imagery is closely associated with vocabulary. When we want to describe something we often use similes:

This cheese is like soap.

or metaphors:

I hissed at him. (Snakes, not people, 'hiss'.)

The comparisons are always significant because they can raise or reduce our respect for the subject matter. If, for example, a poet uses words such as 'bellow' or 'roar' in describing a man, he is being equated with an animal. If a woman is defined in terms of flowers, her beauty is being reinforced, but she is also, perhaps, being seen as an object rather than as a human being.

Preparing an answer on Walcott

There is no set of mechanical rules which we can follow in preparing to answer questions on any writer. The most important thing is to know your texts. Read them aloud; think about them; talk about them; try to understand them. When it comes to answering questions, it is advisable to keep the following points in mind:

(1) Read the question carefully, ensuring that you know exactly what is required of you.
(2) Plan your answer in points before writing your essay. A good essay will have an introductory paragraph devoted to a consideration of the topic, separate paragraphs on each of the points you make, and a concluding paragraph evaluating the topic from your point of view.
(3) Use quotations, even one- or two-word quotations, in support of your opinion.
(4) Write simply, clearly and honestly. There is no particular merit in long sentences and polysyllabic words. Examiners are interested in your response to Derek Walcott, rather than that of teachers or critics.
(5) Always re-read your essays. If you cannot understand what you have written, no one else will.

Sample questions and suggested answers

It is neither useful nor desirable to offer students a set of 'model' answers, since over-reliance on such answers can limit original thinking and discourage students from using their own knowledge creatively. These Notes are intended to train minds, not memories. Nevertheless, it may be helpful to indicate how a student might deal with a topic, and so one full, sample essay is provided, together with two essay plans. If you disagree with some of the points made, that is good, but notice that the subject is dealt with logically and systematically.

Walcott is sometimes described as 'a nature poet'. Say what you think this means by reference to a selection of poems.

Plan

INTRODUCTION:

(*a*)   What is meant by 'a nature poet'?

(*b*)   Nature as natural beauty and a teacher?

(*c*)   Nature 'red in tooth and claw'?

(*d*)   Nature as an uninvolved onlooker?

BODY OF ESSAY:

How does he write about natural phenomena (e.g. 'Ebb', 'Moon', 'The Swamp'), about animals (e.g. 'The Whale, His Bulwark', 'Hawk'), about plants (e.g. 'The Almond Trees')?

CONCLUSION:

Is he 'a nature poet'? Yes, but much more. He writes about nature, about its effect on us and our impact on it and feels that he, as a poet, has a duty to preserve the heritage that existed before our 'race began'.

Essay answer

Often, when people talk about a nature poet, they think of Romantic writers like Wordsworth, who delighted in daffodils:

> Fluttering and dancing in the breeze . . .
> ('I wandered lonely as a cloud')

who claimed that the simplest flower could inspire:

> Thoughts that do often lie too deep for tears . . .
> ('Ode on Intimations of Immortality')

whose heart could 'leap up' when he saw:

> A rainbow in the sky . . .   ('My heart leaps up')

and who felt that nature was a teacher:

The guide, the guardian of my heart, and soul
Of all my moral being.   ('Tintern Abbey')

An extreme view of the Romantic approach to nature has been described as 'the pathetic fallacy'. This belief, that nature reflects our moods, is heard in many popular songs:

When you're crying, you bring on the rain . . .
                                         ('When you're smiling')

and in sentimental verse.

A second view of nature, which Tennyson described as 'red in tooth and claw' (*In Memoriam*, LV) concentrates less on tranquil beauty and more on the merciless power of eagles, hawks and tigers. This is the nature, summed up in Charles Darwin's 'survival of the fittest' phrase and featured in many poems by Ted Hughes.

There is a third view of nature, which is seen, metaphorically, as an uninvolved onlooker. This position is perhaps best summed up by W. H. Auden:

Looking up at the stars, I know quite well
That, for all they care, I can go to hell.
                                       ('The More Loving One')

From this standpoint, nature is neither a benign mother nor a malicious spirit. It is a non-sentient system comprising all natural phenomena, including animal and plant life.

Walcott is aware of these approaches to nature, and they can all be seen in different sections of his work. The sea is an omnipresent symbol of natural beauty in many of his works; he is aware of the darker aspects of nature, of the patient, destructive power of the 'Hawk' and the terror of 'The Swamp'; and, in later poems, such as 'To Return to the Trees', there is a stoical awareness that we must all die and that, although we may find a 'joy beyond lyrical utterance' in natural beauty, it cannot alter our ultimate end 'under the sand'.

There is hardly a poem of Walcott's which does not, in some way, comment on nature. He writes specifically about natural phenomena in such poems as 'Ebb', 'The Swamp' and 'Missing the Sea'. 'Ebb' reminds us that, yearly, we sacrifice our environment and settle for 'the washed-up moon'. 'The Swamp' is described as dark and threatening, something beyond our control, like death or a nightmare. 'Missing the Sea' is a meditation on the loss of something one has always known. The sea was as much a part of his youth as the air in his lungs or the beat of his heart. Its absence is endured like the loss of childhood or of loved ones.

Walcott also writes about animals, especially in 'A Tropical Bestiary', where he philosophises on whale and lizard, octopus and ibis. In 'The

Whale, His Bulwark', the whale symbolises nature's ability to inspire us with awe. We are diminished as a species, if we devalue others' right to existence. Other animal poems, such as 'Hawk', concentrate on the patience of birds of prey and stress the lack of mercy they share with humanity. In writing about animals, Walcott never becomes sentimental. The subject matter of 'Oddjob, a Bull Terrier' is the death of a pet but, in spite of being a moving evocation of the pain of loss, it remains dignified and detached, aware that strongest emotions are best communicated by silence.

Occasionally, Walcott expresses the animal pleasures that children experience when they are close to nature and can run on the hills in the early morning. We find this in 'Allegre', but we also find the adult awareness that the sky can appear most beautiful when it presages drought. A more usual motif in Walcott appears in 'The Castaway'. There is nothing idyllic about the life of the man, stranded on a tropical paradise. Time, space and reality are changed by the enforced loneliness in which:

Cracking a sea-louse, I make thunder split.

Walcott is certainly 'a nature poet'. He writes about nature, about its effect on us and our impact on it and feels that he, as a poet, has a duty to preserve the heritage that existed before our 'race began'. For this poet, however, nature is rarely an end in itself. It symbolises aspects of humanity's struggle. The Gulf of Mexico in 'The Glory Trumpeter' is also the gulf between our aspirations and our achievements; the stars in 'The Harbour' represent the unattainable goals that dedicated artists set themselves; almond trees, that survive and bear fruit in harsh conditions, are like transplanted African women, eternal and indestructable; the fragile beauty of a butterfly is matched by the ephemeral existence of a little girl in 'A Lesson for this Sunday'; 'Ebb' deals not only with the retreat of the sea but with wanton destruction of the environment; and the sea is always itself, eternal and indifferent, but also a reminder of the human cruelty and endurance of 'the middle passage'.

Write a detailed analysis of one poem by Walcott, indicating why you find it both attractive and effective.

For this type of essay, you should select a short poem that you can deal with comprehensively. Try 'The Harbour', 'Allegre', 'Nearing Forty', 'Adam's Song' or 'Earth'. The first four are dealt with in the Summaries of Part 3, so we shall use 'Earth' as the basis for this analysis.

Plan
INTRODUCTION:
What is the significance of the title? What is the general impression of this 19-line poem? Anger? Pain? Stoicism?

BODY OF ESSAY:
You may find it useful to divide this into four paragraphs, each dealing with a specific topic.

(1) Comment on the form of the poem, composed of three-lined stanzas, except for the last stanza which is the one line:

you can never be dispossessed.

Is it rhymed? Is it metrically regular? Are the lines end-stopped? Is alliteration significant? Are you aware of assonance? The poem begins with 'Let . . .' What does this imply? Is it asking for permission (e.g. Let me go)? Is it like the opening of a prayer (e.g. Let us now pray)?

(2) If appropriate, comment on the sentence structure. Are there questions? negatives? commands? suggestions? statements? Are we being *told* something overtly or covertly? Look at the pronouns and at what they imply. Is the speaker identified as 'I' or as an omniscient observer? If 'you' is used, does it refer to the reader or to one or more of the personas in the poem?

(3) Comment on the vocabulary: Are the words simple (e.g. feet) or complex (e.g. vegetal)? Are they concrete (e.g. knuckles) or abstract (e.g. outcry)? Do the words belong to any sets? (Look, for example, at the set associated with the body: feet, knuckles, knees, hair, forehead, veins, armpits, eyelids. Look also at how this human set is associated with a set from inanimate nature: vegetal, stone, tree, moon, silver, rivulets, leaves.) Can you draw any conclusions? Are we all part of life and nature?

(4) Comment on the imagery. This should develop naturally from the section on words. The two main sets of images are of the human body and the natural world. Does the poet use similes (overt comparisons) or metaphors (covert comparisons)? Are there any other figures of speech (e.g. understatement? hyperbole?).

CONCLUSION:
Sum up the points you have made and offer an evaluation of the merits of the poem.

Revision questions

The following questions should help you in your work on the poetry of Derek Walcott.

(1) Walcott's poems often focus on the opposing influences of his African and European heritage. Discuss this conflict as it appears in one or more of his poems.

(2) Describe and discuss Walcott's major skills as a poet.

(3) Derek Walcott frequently writes about suffering and alienation. Does this mean we can classify him as a 'pessimistic' poet? Support your answer by close reference to one or two poems.

(4) 'Derek Walcott is a difficult poet, very hard to understand and appreciate.' Do you agree with this statement? Show by close analysis of two or more poems why it is worth making the effort to overcome the initial difficulties we face.

(5) Illustrate and discuss Walcott's views on love and friendship.

(6) 'The importance of preserving West Indian culture is a prominent theme in Walcott's poetry.' Discuss.

(7) Examine Walcott's preoccupation with one or more of the following motifs: the injustice of colonial rule; the role of the artist in society; the value of history in understanding the present; the sea as a symbol.

(8) 'Walcott's versatility as a poet is enviable. His greatest strength, however, is as a writer of lyrical monologues, in which he himself is the central character.' Examine the above statement, indicating whether or not you agree with the claim.

(9) What is the purpose of the many literary, cultural and religious allusions in Walcott's poetry?

(10) Write an essay on Walcott as a love poet.

Part 5

Suggestions for further reading

Texts

BROWN, STEWART (ED.): *Caribbean Poetry Now*, Hodder and Stoughton, London, 1984.
BROWN, WAYNE (ED.): *Derek Walcott: Selected Poems*, Heinemann, London, 1981; available in paperback. This is the main text used in the preparation of these notes.
BURNETT, PAULA (ED.): *The Penguin Book of Caribbean Verse*, Penguin, Harmondsworth, 1986.

Selected works by Derek Walcott

In a Green Night: Poems 1948–60, Jonathan Cape, London, 1962.
Selected Poems, Farrar, Straus and Co., New York, 1964.
The Castaway and Other Poems, Jonathan Cape, London, 1965.
The Gulf and Other Poems, Jonathan Cape, London, 1969.
Another Life, Farrar, Straus and Giroux, New York, 1973.
Sea Grapes, Jonathan Cape, London, 1976.
The Star-Apple Kingdom, Farrar, Straus and Giroux, New York, 1979.
The Fortunate Traveller, Farrar, Straus and Giroux, New York, 1981.
Midsummer, Farrar, Straus and Giroux, New York, 1984.
Collected Poems 1948–84, Harper Collins, New York, 1986.
The Arkansas Testament, Farrar, Straus and Giroux, New York, 1987.
Omeros, Farrar, Straus and Giroux, New York, 1990.

Criticism

BEDIENT, CALVIN: 'Derek Walcott, Contemporary', *Parnassus: Poetry in Review*, 9.2, Fall/Winter 1981, pp. 31–44.
BICKERTS, SVEN: *The Electric Life: Essays on Modern Poetry*, William Morrow and Co., New York, 1989, esp. pp. 265–72.
BROWN, STEWART (ED.): *The Art of Derek Walcott*, Seren Books, Bridgend, 1991.
DRAPER, JAMES P. (ED.): 'Derek Walcott', *Black Literature Criticism*, Gale Research, Detroit, 1992, pp. 1790–1807.

GOLDSTRAW, IRMA E.: *Derek Walcott: An Annotated Bibliography of His Works*, Garland Publishing, New York and London, 1984.

HAMNER, R. D.: *Derek Walcott*, Twayne Publishers, Boston, 1981.

HEANEY, SEAMUS: 'The Language in Exile', *Parnassus: Poetry in Review*, 8.1, Fall/Winter 1979, pp. 5–11.

O'BRIEN, SEAN: 'In Terms of the Ocean', *The Times Literary Supplement*, 4563, September 14–20, 1990, pp. 977–8.

PEARN, JULIE: *Poetry in the Caribbean*, Hodder and Stoughton, London, 1985.

SAAKANA, AMON SABA: *The Colonial Legacy in Caribbean Literature*, Vol. 1, Karnak House, London, 1987.

TAYLOR, PATRICK: 'Myth and Reality in Caribbean Narrative: Derek Walcott's *Pantomime*', *World Literature Written in English*, 26.1, Spring 1986, pp. 169–77.

Index

The index gives an alphabetical listing of the poems discussed in Part 3.

The author of these notes

LORETO TODD is Reader in International English at the University of Leeds. Educated in Northern Ireland and England, she has degrees in English Language, Literature and Linguistics. Dr Todd has taught in England and in West Africa, and has lectured in Australia, Canada, the Caribbean, Europe, Papua New Guinea, Singapore and the United States of America. She has published numerous articles and reviews, a dictionary, twenty books, including *International English Usage* (1990) and *Variety in Contemporary English* (1991), and is an associate editor of the *Oxford Companion to the English Language* (1992). At present, she is engaged in a study of the language of literature.